CW00371519

THE LINGUISTIC CONSTRUCTION OF REALITY

THE LINGUISTIC CONSTRUCTION OF REALITY

George W. Grace

CROOM HELM
London • New York • Sydney

© 1987 George W. Grace
Croom Helm Publishers Ltd, Provident House,
Burrell Row, Beckenham, Kent, BR3 1AT
Croom Helm Australia, 44 – 50 Waterloo Road,
North Ryde, 2113, New South Wales

British Library Cataloguing in Publication Data

   The linguistic construction of reality.
   1. Psycholinguistics   2. Reality
   3. Perception
   I. Title
   153.7   BF455
   ISBN 0 – 7099 – 3886 – 1

Published in the USA by
Croom Helm
in association with Methuen, Inc.
29 West 35th Street
New York, NY 10001

Library of Congress Cataloging-in-Publication Data

Grace, George William, 1921-
   The linguistic construction of reality.

   Bibliography: p.
   Includes index.
   1. Languages — Philosphy. 2. Sapir-Whorf hypothesis.
I. Title.
P106.G66 1987   401   87-15915
ISBN 0-7099-3886-1

Printed and bound in Great Britain
by Billing & Sons Limited, Worcester.

Contents

Part I: Views of Language

1. The Mapping and Reality-construction Views of Language   3

2. Subject-matter Views   16

Part II: Saying Things: Conceptual Events

3. Saying Things   25

4. Conceptual Events and Real-world Situations   41

5. The Problem of Translation   55

Part III: Conceptual Worlds

6. Conceptual Elements   75

7. Ways of Talking about Things   92

8. Conceptual Worlds   108

Part IV: Further Implications

9. The Question of the Relation Between Language and Thought   117

10. The Question of Individual Linguistic Competence   125

Concluding Remarks   139

References Cited   144

Index   149

Part I

Views of Language

1

The Mapping and Reality-construction Views of Language

It has been said that sciences create their own objects of study. There is an important sense in which that is true, and in this book we will be considering how it is true specifically of the science of language — linguistics. But this creation of their objects by the sciences is only one aspect of the more general phenomenon which has been referred to as 'the social construction of reality'.[1] Those who speak of our reality as socially constructed are emphasizing the part played by cultural constructs in our effective environment — our environment as we perceive it and respond to it (as contrasted with the part played by the actual characteristics of the external environment itself). The point is that the *effective* environment of human beings is more cultural than natural.

The human species — and no other — possesses the one essential tool which makes a social construction of reality possible. That tool is language. Not only is language the means by which this kind of reality construction is accomplished, it is also the means by which the realities, once constructed, are preserved and transmitted from person to person and from generation to generation. Hence, it is entirely appropriate to refer more specifically to the *linguistic* construction of reality.

The point here is that any group of humans discussing any subject matter quickly arrives at a way of looking at — and *talking about* — that subject matter which very much influences everything they subsequently do or say about it. Both the isolation of particular objects of investigation as objects and the characteristics which are attributed to them once they are isolated are aspects of this creation of objects, of this 'reality construction'. Both the definition of the subject matter in the first place and the way in

3

which it is viewed (what it is perceived as being *like*) once it has been defined are products of reality construction.

It would seem apparent that since our reality construction — the creation of our views of things — is carried out by means of language, our best prospect for understanding how reality construction is accomplished must be through studying how language works.

Unfortunately, at this point we encounter an obstacle; our acknowledged science of language, i.e. linguistics, is committed to a view of language which makes it very difficult to study this aspect of the way in which language works. In fact, not only does this accepted view of language make it difficult to design and carry out research on the reality-constructing function of language, it makes it difficult even to acknowledge that such reality construction occurs at all.

This brings us to a key point. It is particularly important to keep constantly in mind that our customary way of viewing language is *itself* the product of such reality construction. That is, our society has a particular perspective on language, a particular way of looking at it and talking about it. This view of language is represented quite clearly in linguistics, the acknowledged 'science of language', but our society at large seems to hold essentially the same view. Because this view so permeates our institutions, it is important to emphasize that there is nothing necessary about it — that there is nothing in the nature of language itself which compels us to this view of it. To give a name to this view of language, let us call it the *mapping view*. The reasons for this choice of name will become clear later.

The title of this book, *The Linguistic Construction of Reality*, implies a quite different view of language, a quite different conception of what kind of thing language is and of how it works. The book will be devoted to developing that view, which may appropriately be called the *reality construction* view.

I will try to show that the differences between the mapping and the reality-construction views of language are fundamental ones with far-reaching implications. In fact, it is difficult to imagine any conception of the nature of language, unless it is so shallow as not to be worthy of the name, which does not have far-reaching implications. It is difficult, in short, to imagine a view of language which does not carry with it epistemological assumptions — assumptions about the nature of the world, or at least of our access to knowledge of the world.

4

Although the mapping view (in one form or another) seems clearly to be the standard view of language today, the reader should not get the impression that the reality-construction view is something which was just made up for the purpose of this book and which is without historical antecedents. On the contrary, its roots go back a very long way, and there are numerous important historical figures who could reasonably be reckoned as having contributed to its development.[2] Names which might be mentioned include Etienne Bonnet de Condillac (who said that every science is a well-made language), Destutt de Tracy and the *idéologues*, Wilhelm von Humboldt, and most recently Benjamin Lee Whorf (although even a very superficial historical review would yield many other names).

How fundamentally incompatible the two views are was illustrated by the revival of the reality-construction view through the reprinting of some of the writings of Whorf in 1950 and 1956.[3] There was simply no way for them to be discussed from the standpoint of standard linguistic theory.

(The ultimate disposition of Whorf's ideas was approximately as follows. Within a short time, linguistics seemed to settle upon a common position with regard to Whorf's writings, a position which was widely accepted beyond the confines of the linguistic profession as well. The crux of that position is that what Whorf was actually proposing was some kind of *hypothesis* about a relation between language and perception (or world view, or thought, or culture), but that he had given no clear formulation of this supposed hypothesis and that no one else has ever been able to do so either. That is, no one else has been able to figure out how to formulate it so that it can be tested. As a consequence, it is in terms of hypothesis formulation and testing that Whorfianism is now conventionally discussed. Thus, the unofficial position of the profession is essentially that Whorf had some challenging ideas, but that there is no way to subject them to a scientific test, and that, therefore, unless some unforeseeable breakthrough occurs, there is nothing further which can be done with them.)

Two Views of Language

The principal differences between the mapping and reality-construction views of language all seem to be traceable to different conceptions of the way in which languages represent reality —

different conceptions of the relation between a language and external reality. Thus, it may be said that the basic differences between the two views are attributable to the different epistemological assumptions underlying them.

The basic epistemological assumption of the mapping view might be stated as follows: there is a common world out there and our languages are analogous to maps of this world. Thus, this common world is represented or 'mapped' (with greater or less distortion) by all languages.[4] Advocates of the mapping view acknowledge that each language provides a somewhat different mapping. However, the differences are assumed to be due at least in part to the fact that, since our access to knowledge of this world is imperfect, different peoples (speaking different languages) have arrived at slightly different understandings of it. The differences in details from the mapping of one language to that of another may be thought of as differences in the way they 'divide the common world up' — in the way they 'classify' its phenomena.

In the *reality-construction* view, the imperfectness of our access to knowledge of the real world assumes central importance. Emphasis is placed upon the fact that we do not have direct access to the real world itself, but only to the data about it provided by our senses. And these senses provide very incomplete information. Our eyes, for example, respond only to a very narrow band of wavelengths within the electromagnetic spectrum, our ears only to a certain limited range of vibratory frequencies in the air or some other medium, etc.

Thus, in the reality-construction view, our sensory data are regarded as falling seriously short of constituting an adequate picture of the real world. They are considered to be very incomplete and unsystematic, are seen as not adding up to anything like a representative sample of what is out there. On the contrary, all we can do (according to this view) is invent explanations for the sensory data which are attempts to make sense of the whole of the sensory input. To put it differently, all we can do is to theorize about reality, or to put it more precisely still, to construct models of it. These models are our constructed realities, and they are reflected in the languages we speak.

Of course, these constructed realities are not assumed to be fabricated out of the whole cloth. The real world imposes some constraints. The experiences of people in different cultures are not assumed to be totally random with respect to one another.

However, once this concession has been made, it might seem

that there is really no significant difference between the mapping view and the reality-construction view. In the mapping view, although what languages are regarded as ultimately representing is a real world — an objective reality the existence of which is independent of any observers — it is nevertheless acknowledged that different languages do have a great deal of latitude as to how they divide up and interpret that world. And in the reality-construction view, although the representations provided by our languages are regarded as nothing more than models which serve as surrogates for the real world, it is nevertheless acknowledged that these models are constrained by the nature of the real world as we encounter it. It might seem, therefore, that there is no disagreement about the facts and that the only difference is a difference of emphasis.

However, in reality, differences of emphasis can be most important — fully as important as differences of empirical fact and even much more so. What is really important is what questions are effectively askable by those who take a particular view as their point of departure. The important differences between basic views of language (or of any other subject matter) are in what is regarded as problematic and what is taken for granted. The most basic assumptions of any such view are, in effect, incorrigible (i.e. not subject to correction in the light of subsequent experience). The reason for this is that there is no natural way in which they could be disconfirmed since the question of their truthfulness could not naturally arise within the framework in question.

The Mapping View

But there is one key assumption, in particular, which may be thought of as containing in a nutshell the essence of the entire mapping view of language. That is the assumption that 'anything can be said in any language' — that is, that any content that can be expressed in one language can be expressed in any other language. We may refer to this assumption as the *intertranslatability postulate*.[5] It is easy to see how this postulate arises out of the mapping view's assumption that all languages are mappings of a common world, and that anything that can be said in any language ultimately refers back to this common world. Given this assumption, all languages and all things that can be said in any of them must be commensurable because this universally-shared world is their common measure.

The intertranslatability postulate has important implications for the nature of language and of individual languages. It implies, for example, that each language is an empty code — a code which is entirely uncommitted as to content and for which any conceivable subject matter constitutes potential content. Each language is thus by its nature a *universal encoder*.

The mapping view seems to lead inevitably to a quite surprising conclusion — the conclusion that languages, or at any rate their individual features, are irrelevant to anything except other features of the same languages. It seems surprising, to say the least, that the science of language should willingly have embraced a view which so belittles the role of language in human life. This seeming antipathy of the profession to its own best interests traces back, I believe, to its deep commitment to establishing and maintaining its autonomy.

In its pursuit of autonomy, linguistics (through its spokesmen) has insisted upon the independence of language from everything else. In pursuing this strategy it has willingly embraced the assumption that the features of a particular language — those features of which a linguistic description is constituted — are non-adaptive with respect to everything in the extra-linguistic environment. That is (except for vocabulary, which (*nota bene*) is not regarded as a central part of the language system), it is assumed that no feature of any language is better adapted to any aspect of the extra-linguistic environment than would be any different feature which might have occurred in its place.

Because of this presumed non-adaptiveness, linguistics can analyze the synchronic structure of a language without considering anything extra-linguistic — without considering anything beyond the kinds of features which figure in linguistic descriptions. Likewise, they can comfortably pursue the study of linguistic change without regard to anything except the languages themselves (as these languages are represented by their linguistic descriptions). The linguistic features of a language, then — those features which are reported in linguistic descriptions — must be non-adaptive. And non-adaptive means *irrelevant* as far as any considerations beyond those which are regarded as linguistic in the strict sense are concerned. Linguistics, in other words, has become committed to the irrelevance of what it studies (except for whatever universal principles emerge from these studies) to anything external to language, and reciprocally, to the irrelevance of anything external to language to what linguistics studies.

But this 'mapping' view of language has further ramifications. The intertranslatability postulate and the assumption that languages are universal encoders lead naturally to several further assumptions about the nature of language. I will describe some of them.

First of all, unless, we want to deny that different cultures exhibit differences in their concepts, beliefs, and values, we must conclude that cultures (since they exhibit such differences) are sharply distinguished from their associated languages (since in the universal-encoder view, languages cannot be subject to any differences of that kind).

Thus we are led to the assumption that a language and its accompanying culture are quite separate and distinct entities.[6]

Secondly, to say that all languages can represent exactly the same range of content seems to be just another way of saying that all languages can express the same range of thoughts. Once that is assumed to be true, then it seems to follow that the basic processes of thought are clearly separated from language (or at the very least from those characteristics of languages which are not universal but which can differ from one language to another).

Thus we are led to the assumption that the basic processes of thought are quite independent of our languages.

Thirdly, it seems to follow almost necessarily from the propositions so far stated that what can be said, and therefore what can be talked about, is fixed once and for all. Not only does the intertranslatability postulate require that the set of 'things' which can be said be the same for all languages, it also requires that this set can never be altered in any way for any language. Therefore, according to the intertranslatability postulate the set of sayable things must necessarily have remained fixed since the beginning of human languages (or at least of intertranslatable languages).

Thus we are implicitly commited to the strong ontological assumption that there is an objectively given world common to all people which defines for all time what can be talked about.

Finally (this may seem of secondary importance to some, but I attribute a great deal of importance to it), since in the universal-encoder conception of languages all languages are functionally equivalent, it seems to follow that nothing would be lost if the present linguistic diversity in the world were replaced by a single universal language.

Thus we are led to the assumption that the world would have everything to gain and nothing to lose if there were a single language spoken by everyone, and, in fact, that there would be no harm done if this universal language were the only language which survived.

The Reality-construction View

I do not at all believe that these assumptions about the irrelevance of a language to everything else and of everything else to the language are actually true. In fact, not only do I believe that they are quite false, but I also believe that they constitute a serious obstacle to progress in learning what language is really like and how it affects various aspects of our daily lives and of human existence. To illustrate something of what is at stake, I will propose an alternative set of assumptions. These assumptions represent my version of the 'reality-construction' view. I believe that they are a much more accurate reflection of the real nature of language and its role in our affairs.

The reality-construction view of language may be defined by the following assumptions:

1) That what is said cannot in any satisfactory way be separated from the way in which it is said.

2) That no clear boundary in terms of their functions can be drawn between the 'structure' of a language and its vocabulary, and therefore that the grammars of different languages are no more functionally equivalent to one another than are the languages as wholes.

3) That a language is shaped by its culture, and a culture is given expression in its language, to such an extent that it is impossible to say where one ends and the other begins, i.e. what belongs to language and what to culture.

4) That it is impossible to draw a clear line between thinking, i.e. bringing a thought into being, and encoding the thought, i.e. putting it into words.

5) That what can be said, and what can be talked about, may be quite different from one language-culture system to another.

6) That (this being so) it is likely that the potentialities have not been exhausted yet, that new language-culture systems are theoretically possible which will have significantly different views of the world from any existing today — which will talk about things that we cannot dream of now.

10

7) That it is misleading to talk without proper qualification of human beings as all living in a common objectively given world; that each language-culture system must to some extent have its own conceptual world that is the product of its own history — a world that has been created continuously by its speakers throughout that history.

8) That (in view of the last two points) the details of the adaptation of the human species are not as completely dictated by the nature of reality as some have been inclined to suppose.

9) That, therefore, there is no reason to believe that other worlds with natural environments similar to earth would, even given unlimited time, evolve 'intelligent beings' with languages intertranslatable with ours.

10) That, since different languages are not functionally equivalent, the prospect of the present linguistic diversity in the world being submerged by a single juggernaut of a language (say English) is at least as disturbing as the prospect of the extinction of biological species, and the suggestion that diverse languages might maintain what is essential to their true individuality while some artificial international language (such as Esperanto) insures effective intercultural communication totally misunderstands and misrepresents the nature of language.

Conclusions

I expect that most well-informed people, including most linguists, would agree that the assumptions of the second set — corresponding to the reality-construction view of language — are more believable than those of the first set (or at least that the more basic ones are). However, I also expect that most of the same people, and especially most linguists, will at the same time talk and act *as if* they subscribed to the assumptions of the first set. There may appear to be a contradiction in such behavior, but that is only because we fail to distinguish between making assumptions and holding beliefs. As the next chapter will attempt to demonstrate more clearly, they are in reality two different matters.

We seem, therefore, to be faced with two sharply conflicting views of the nature of language and the way in which language functions. In particular, a key assumption of the reality-construction view of language is that it is *not* the case that anything which can be said in one language can also be said in any other language.

11

To be more explicit, the assumption of the reality-construction view is that there is no coherent interpretation which can be made of the postulate by which it could conceivably be true and by which it would still be compatible with various of the institutions which we have built upon the assumption that translation is always possible. That is to say that, according to the reality-construction view, what we are calling the intertranslatability postulate is false.

Now it might seem that in a case where directly opposed claims have been asserted, the natural course would be to proceed immediately to an empirical test to determine which was correct. However, to expect empirical testing would be to misunderstand how science (or at least what, in disciplines such as linguistics, is called science) works.

Postulates such as the intertranslatability postulate are not intended as empirical hypotheses. They are more comparable to articles of faith in that they are incorrigible within the scholarly traditions to which they belong. It seems likely that the principal value of the intertranslatability postulate to the present version of linguistics is that it provides the justification for the Carnapian concept of syntactical structure — that is, the notion that there are structures composed purely of signs in systematic relations with other signs. It provides that justification because it carries the clear implication that all languages, once one abstracts from their vocabularies, are functionally equivalent. To reject the intertranslatability postulate might, therefore, ultimately remove the justification for such key subject-matter areas of linguistics as syntax and phonology. That would pretty much amount to rejecting the whole paradigm of linguistics as it now stands.

But it might not be necessary to reject the intertranslatability postulate, and therefore the mapping view of language, entirely. There are two reasons for saying this. The first reason is that the intertranslatability postulate is quite vague (as befits a scientific postulate). Although I will try to show that in what seems to be its most natural interpretation it is false, the possibility that it could be given some other fairly precise interpretation by which it would be true will not have been excluded.

The second reason is that even if it should prove to be incorrect under all reasonable interpretations, there is no objection to incorrect assumptions as such; in fact, it seems reasonable to suppose that incorrect assumptions are necessary to any 'scientific' study.[8] The kind of incorrect assumptions that prove useful are likely to be not so much outright falsehoods as over-simplifications, but some such assumptions are regularly necessary for the kind of investigation which is thought of as scientific. The reason appears to be that without them it is impossible to formulate sufficiently precise questions for investigation. And questions have to be precise if it is to be possible to design a strategy for answering them.

The fate of the mapping view, therefore, should be made to depend upon a demonstration that its assumptions provide a more useful basis for the investigation of certain types of phenomena than does any alternative set of assumptions. This view, in fact, appears to have been designed from the outset with one specific application in mind — application to problems connected with the use of language for information processing. It might well be preserved as the basis for a linguistics (that would then frankly be acknowledged to be an 'applied' linguistics) consecrated to such purposes.

Of course, none of what has just been said is intended to suggest that the mapping view provides a sufficient basis for learning what we need to know about the nature of language. On the contrary, this book will attempt to show that the mapping view in the long run conceals more than it reveals about the nature of language and the role of language and language differences in a wide range of human affairs. It will attempt to show how a generally more revealing view of language — what we are here calling the 'reality-construction' view — can be developed in a satisfactory way.

Notes

1. *The Social Construction of Reality* is the title of a widely cited book by Peter L. Berger and Thomas Luckmann, which has appeared in various editions (cf. Berger and Luckmann 1966).

2. With my very limited knowledge of the prominent thinkers of the seventeenth, eighteenth and nineteenth centuries, it is difficult for me to be precise as to exactly which of them should be counted as adhering to the reality-construction view of language or as having views which contributed to its development. However, it seems obvious that a number of them held views which were relatively close to that which I develop in this book. Of the historical treatments which I know of, Aarsleff 1982 comes closest to isolating the tradition which I have in mind.

3. The work of Benjamin Lee Whorf came into prominence through the re-publication of four of the articles which most strongly advocated his reality-construction views (Whorf 1950). A much larger collection was Carroll 1956. Hoijer 1954 consists of the proceedings of a conference devoted essentially to Whorf's ideas. Feuer 1953 and Lenneberg 1953 as well as some of the contributions to Hoijer 1954 have been among the

more influential criticisms of Whorf's ideas.

4. An extreme version of the 'mapping view' is the notion of 'Adamic language' (i.e. the language of Adam), which Hans Aarsleff (1982: 25) describes as 'the most widely held seventeenth-century view of the nature of language'. George Steiner (1975: 58) wrote of it:

> The vulgate of Eden contained, though perhaps in a muted key, a divine syntax — powers of statement and designation analogous to God's own diction, in which the mere naming of a thing was the necessary and sufficient cause of its leap into reality. Each time man spoke he re-enacted, he mimed, the nominalist mechanism of creation.

In the doctrine of Adamic language, of course, the relation between signifier and signified is not arbitrary. But even in the seventeenth century, in spite of the multiplicity and seemingly chaos of languages of that time, it was held that they retained 'the divine nature of their common origin', and that they 'were in fundamental accord with nature, indeed they were themselves part of creation and nature' (Aarsleff 1982: 25).

What has made this doctrine from the seventeenth century of particular significance for us is that that is precisely the era in which modern science was taking shape, and, as Richard Rorty (1979: 387) reminds us, 'the assumptions that scientific discourse was normal discourse and that all other discourses needed to be modeled upon it' have persisted in philosophy since 'the period of Descartes and Hobbes'. I think there can be no question that linguistics' view of the nature of language has been taken over without serious scrutiny from philosophy and that its view of language clearly represents an idealized scientific language.

And at the time when modern science was taking shape, a return to something approximating Adamic language was regarded as a realistic objective. In the words of Murray Cohen (1977: xxiii), 'For everyone concerned with language in the middle of the seventeenth century, it seemed possible to organize, recover, or invent a language that represented the order of things in the world'. That even as late as 1938, Charles W. Morris was able to refer to the theory that 'languages mirror (correspond with, reflect, are isomorphic with) the realm of nonlinguistic objects' as 'one of the oldest and most persistent theories' (Morris 1938: 26) suggests that the influence of the Adamic language doctrine is far from disappearing.

In recent times, philosophers of science have striven diligently to find a way in which language can be regarded as 'hooking onto' the real world — a prominent example being the notion of 'operational definition' proposed by Percy W. Bridgman — but as the present book will attempt to show, that objective is unrealistic.

Michael J. Reddy's paper, 'The conduit metaphor — a case of frame conflict in our language about language' (Reddy 1979), most effectively illustrates how some of the assumptions of what I call the 'mapping' view as well as various others are incorporated in our way of talking about language.

5. The following are some statements gleaned from the literature, which represent essentially what we are calling the intertranslatability postulate:

14

1) Eric H. Lenneberg 1953: 467: 'A basic maxim in linguistics is that anything can be expressed in any language.'

2) Edward Sapir (in Mandelbaum 1949: 153): '. . . we may say that a language is so constructed that no matter what any speaker of it may desire to communicate, no matter how original or bizarre his idea or fancy, the language is prepared to do his work.'

3) John B. Carroll 1953: 47: 'In general (that is, aside from differences arising from culture and technology), contrary to the popularly held misconception, anything that can be said in one language can be said in any other language.'

4) Osgood and Sebeok 1954: 193 (from a section attributed to Donald E. Walker, James J. Jenkins, and Thomas A. Sebeok): 'This comes out clearly in statements such as "anything *can* be expressed in any language, but the structure of a given language will favor certain statements and hinder others".'

5) John R. Searle 1969: 19: 'The principle that whatever can be meant can be said, which I shall refer to as the "principle of expressibility", is important for the subsequent argument of this book.'

6) Jerrold J. Katz 1976: 37 (his so-called 'effability' principle): 'Every proposition is the sense of some sentence in each natural language.'

6. A frequently-cited statement of the mutual independence of language and culture is found in Sapir 1921: 221–35.

7. What I call here the 'Carnapian concept of syntactical structure' is part of a scheme of logicians in which the central structure is a system of relations of signs to signs. That system is known as syntactics. Other systems are constituted of the relations of signs to the objects to which they can refer (semantics), and the relations of signs to the language users (pragmatics). However, 'pragmatics' now seems to be evolving into a more general term for everything (which is, of course, an enormous amount) that syntactics and semantics leave out. The most familiar source, at least to linguists, on the syntactics-semantics-pragmatics scheme is Morris 1938.

8. Note that when I say that incorrect assumptions may be necessary to any scientific study, 'scientific' is intended to imply the 'hypothetico-deductive method' and not to include Northrop's (1947) 'natural history stage' of inquiry.

2

Subject-matter Views

The main argument of this book is that the particular subject-matter view which informs the current paradigm of linguistics is responsible for the failure of linguistics to investigate the formation and maintenance of, precisely, subject-matter views. But surely their investigation falls within the responsibilities of linguistics, if linguistics is concerned with understanding the nature of language. For, as is argued throughout this book, the assumptions which are conventionally made — the assumptions which constitute our subject-matter views — are an important by-product of language; or even more, perhaps they should not be regarded as a by-product at all, but indeed as the most important consequence of our possession of language. If that is true, it would seem to follow that any serious inquiry into the nature of language would have to study the role of such assumptions in determining the characteristics and use of particular languages and the role of language in conventionalizing assumptions.

In any case, since such studies have not been made, not much is known about subject-matter views, and yet it is precisely two contrasting subject-matter views — the mapping and reality-construction views of language — which constitute the subject of this book. Therefore before going on to consider the reality-construction view of language in more detail, it might be well to pause to make a few tentative observations on this obscure topic — the nature of subject-matter views.

Subject-matter Views

As we have seen in the case of the two views of language, subject-

16

matter views can be analyzed into sets of assumptions made about the subject matter in question. The point has been made repeatedly that research in the sciences always presupposes a common set of assumptions among the participating scientists, and further that these assumptions taken together constitute a particular view of the world as a whole and of the particular part of the world which has been selected to constitute the subject matter of the discipline in question.[1] It is this characteristic of sciences which is envisaged in the dictum that sciences create their own objects. Although we are referring to such views here as 'subject-matter' views, it should be understood that they always go far beyond the subject matter of the discipline in the narrow sense. They typically include assumptions about the relation of that subject matter to the world in general and assumptions about epistemology.

Each scientific discipline may be thought of as maintaining an ongoing discourse, which is, in fact, the most important output of that discipline. These ongoing discourses — the discursive traditions of the individual disciplines — are effectively governed by the respective subject-matter views of the particular disciplines. From another perspective, we may observe that it is in these ongoing discourses that the particular subject-matter views are manifested and that is in the contributions by individual scientists to the discourses that these views evolve over time.

Although it is the role which subject-matter views play in the *sciences* that has received the greatest amount of attention, their role is by no means restricted to the sciences. In fact, such (ordinarily tacit) prior agreement on assumptions is a prerequisite for anything approaching normal discourse on any subject to be possible at any time. It is virtually impossible to discuss a subject with anyone who has not previously been aware of the existence of that subject (*qua* subject). When confronted with such a person who is not cognizant of the relevant reality construction, it is necessary first to provide him/her with the key assumptions composing the standard view of the subject, i.e. to teach him/her the conventions of the particular discourse.

Another difficult situation arises when the subject under discussion is understood by both interlocutors to be the same subject, but the ways in which they are accustomed to talking about it reflect different views of it — that is, when more or less different realities have been constructed to represent what purports to be the same real-world object. The immediately relevant example is the two views of 'language' (i.e. two different constructed objects which are both referred to as 'language') being discussed in this book. The confrontation of different views of 'the same' object has been discussed particularly with respect to the problem as it arises during the course of a scientific revolution.[2]

Although these subject-matter views are very important in the functioning of any science and, in fact, in all human discourse, it is usually very difficult to give a precise description of any particular view of this kind. There seem to be at least three reasons for this difficulty. First, such a view is not completely uniform for all of those who subscribe to it (participate in the particular discourse which it generates). We may call non-uniform systems of this sort 'open' systems. Thus, claims about what assumptions a particular tradition makes may be rejected by some on the grounds that the assumptions in question are not uniformly valid for all of the adherents of the tradition. Secondly, people tend to imagine that to assert of particular propositions that they represent assumptions of a particular discursive tradition is tantamount to asserting that these propositions represent beliefs of the individual adherents of that tradition. Thus, claims about the assumptions of a tradition may be rejected on the grounds that they are not what some or all of the adherents of the tradition really believe. Thirdly, such views always remain largely implicit, and it is probably a necessary part of their function that they should do so. We will briefly consider each of those three points.

Subject-matter Views as Open Systems

As was just mentioned, such a view will not be uniform for all of the individuals who are to be thought of as its adherents. However, that should not be considered too serious an obstacle. For example, the same situation obtains with respect to another kind of entity — the entities which we call 'languages', such as the English language. The rules of the English language are not identical from one speaker to another any more than are the assumptions of the members of a particular scholarly tradition.

The fact that it is not possible to give a precise set of rules for the English language which are exactly valid for all speakers of English is not generally taken as requiring the conclusion that there is no English language. No more should the fact that it is not possible to give a precise formulation of assumptions which can be attributed, in that exact formulation, to all members of the school or discipline be taken to mean that there is no sharing of assumptions.

Both systems of assumptions, on the one hand, and languages, on the other, are systems of a kind which we may think of as 'open' systems. That is, they are systems which do not have clear boundaries — where some things belong to the system more clearly than do some others and still others may not belong at all, although there is no (non-arbitrary) basis for saying for sure. In the case of language descriptions, the problem which this openness poses is usually not regarded as being as great, because linguists have worked out various conventions for making descriptive decisions in spite of the internal diversity. However, it should be equally possible to establish comparable conventions for the description of subject-matter views if we were sufficiently desirous of doing so.

Assumptions vs. Personal Beliefs

A point which needs to be emphasized is that the assumptions of subject-matter views are not to be confused with personal *beliefs*. Confusion between the assumptions of a scholarly tradition and the beliefs of its adherents has been the source of much misunderstanding and obfuscation.

Ways of talking about something are overt; the style — the jargon — of a particular scholarly tradition is usually quite conspicuous and easy to identify. Therefore, it is easy to observe whether or not different people talk about a thing in the same way, and it is natural for ways of talking about a thing to become more or less standardized and conventionalized. New adherents to a tradition must learn to speak its language. In fact, a professional level of competence in the use of its way of talking is probably the main ability which they must demonstrate in order to qualify for membership.

It is probably fair to say that when someone new learns a conventional way of talking about something, he/she is learning what the senior people *appear* to believe about it. However, what they appear to believe should be kept distinct from what they actually believe. Furthermore, we should not let ourselves be distracted by the conventional wisdom which would hold that what one actually believes about something is more important than one's way of talking about it.[3] That may be valid if we are concerned with the psychology of the individual taken alone, but if we are interested in the assumptions of a scholarly tradition, the way the participating

19

scholars talk about the object of their discipline is more important for our purposes than what they may believe about it.

Therefore, I say that, except to someone concerned with the state of our psyche, it does not so much matter what we actually believe about a thing; that what matters is what we talk *as if* we believed. The 'mapping' view of language, then, is not being proposed as representing the beliefs of linguists or of anyone else, but rather as assumptions of linguistics as a scholarly tradition (and to a great extent also of the general public in our society).

Inexplicitness of Assumptions

As I pointed out earlier a third reason why it is hard to give a clear description of a subject-matter view is that such views are never made fully explicit. There are probably two principal reasons for this: first, the constituent assumptions were probably not explicit even at the time when they were first adopted, and secondly, the functions which they serve may be better served if they remain inexplicit.

The first point was that it is not likely that there was any explicit agreement by the members of the discipline to most of the constituent assumptions even when the view was in the process of being adopted. What is more likely to have been the case is that at some time in the past some one began talking *as if* such and such things were true. In good time others followed the lead, accepting some of the same terms and metaphors and adding more of their own, until eventually a full-fledged jargon of the familiar sort came into being.

The second point was that such assumptions probably serve their function better if they are not made explicit. That is, it is probably dysfunctional for them to be revealed, because the very functions which they fulfill probably require that they be protected from exposure. If they were revealed, some would surely prove to be false. Now, admittedly it is not the function of such assumptions to be true: their function is to get some basic problems out of the way so that the scientists can focus their attention on the questions that they want to work on. But if the existence of a patently false assumption is disclosed, then attention must inevitably be diverted back to it, and it will become a distraction rather than continue to perform its function.

Therefore, even though there is actually nothing wrong or

unexpected about a science being based on false assumptions,[4] having the falsity of one's assumptions exposed could result in a great deal of inconvenience. This no doubt explains why it seems, from what I have observed, that attempts to specify the assumptions behind a particular subject-matter view are likely to be met with resistance, at the very least, from the adherents of that view.

Notes

1. Probably the best known discussion of the role of assumptions in scholarly traditions (and in this case, specifically in the sciences) is that of Thomas S. Kuhn (cf. Kuhn 1970). His concept of 'paradigm' is now a familiar one. I particularly like the term 'picture of the world' used by Niles Eldredge and Stephen Jay Gould (Eldredge and Gould 1972). That suggested my term 'views' (of subject matters).

2. The classical work on scientific revolutions is of course that of Kuhn (cf. Kuhn 1970).

3. It was Whorf who made me suddenly realize that it is our way of *talking* about the subject which is crucial (cf. Carroll 1956: 220). But Berger and Luckmann's (1966) discussion of the role of ways of talking in reality maintenance (showing how what we say implies a whole world in which saying that particular thing makes sense) also helps to complete the picture. And Rorty (1979) with his concept of 'normal discourse' contributes the additional important point that Kuhn's paradigms are maintained and passed on primarily through their associated ways of talking.

4. Note again that when I say that incorrect assumptions may be necessary to any scientific study, 'scientific' is intended to imply the 'hypothetico-deductive method' and not to include Northrop's (1947) 'natural history stage' of inquiry.

Part II

Saying Things: Conceptual Events

3

Saying Things

Part II is concerned with reality construction in language use, and most particularly, with examining the validity of the intertranslatability postulate. As was pointed out in the first chapter, it appears that all of the differences in the assumptions of the two views of language described there can be traced to the acceptance of the intertranslatability postulate by the mapping view and its rejection by the reality-construction view. Therefore, a detailed examination of what is involved in translatability is warranted.

According to the intertranslatability postulate, anything which can be said in one language can be said in any other language. In order to consider the validity of this claim we must first obtain answers to two questions. The first is: What is the nature of what we may call a 'sayable thing'? That is, when we say 'things', what is the nature of these 'things'? Or again, in what terms is the 'meaning' (or 'content') of a linguistic expression to be characterised? The second is: On what basis are we to say that two sayable things are 'the same'? This chapter will be devoted to answering the first question and the following chapter will begin consideration of the second.

Let us begin by considering the mapping view in more detail to show what answers it would provide for these questions. One version of the mapping view would give an account something like the following:

The real world is a closed system, or near enough to being one for us to act as if it were. That is, there is a single finite real world which is common to all of mankind and, therefore, to the speakers of all languages. Any given language is a way of classifying everything that belongs to that real world: it is therefore analogous to a map. That is, the relation that exists between that language and the real world is analogous to the relation between a map and the territory which it maps. This analogy is found in the fact that the language (mainly by means of its vocabulary) divides up the real world in much the way that a political map divides up the earth's surface — it represents an exhaustive partition of reality.

Each political unit which appears on a map corresponds to a defined territory. Analogously, a lexical item in a particular language corresponds to a certain territory within the real world. The territory to which it corresponds encompasses just the set of real-world phenomena to which it may properly refer. Therefore, it follows that a word can be defined by giving an exact specification of the boundaries of the real-world territory which it represents.

Each language has also a system of syntactic rules which provide for the combination of lexical items to produce sentences. The meaning of a sentence can also be thought of as corresponding to a definable territory within the real world. This territory consists of all of the real-world situations to which the linguistic expression could truly refer. Differently put, the territory is defined to include all of the combinations of real-world conditions under which the expression would be true. In this view translation from one language to another is essentially a matter of expressing the same points in reality in terms of the categories of the second map rather than those of the first.

From the above account we can determine the mapping-view answers to the questions posed above. The first question was: When we say 'things' what is the nature of these 'things', or, In what terms is the content of a linguistic expression to be characterized? The mapping view's answer is that that content consists of the set of real-world situations to which the expression can truly refer, or of the conditions which a situation must meet in order to belong to that set.

The second question was: On what basis are we to say that the content of two different linguistic expressions is the same? The mapping view's answer to that is that their content is the same, if the set of real-world situations to which each may truly refer is the same.

Now, what is probably the most serious error in this view of language is that it conceives of linguistic expressions as if their relation to real-world situations were an immediate one. That is, it attributes to the linguistic expression the qualities of what has been called 'autonomous text', which is to say that it assumes that the expression so specifies its own meaning that it is completely understandable without reference to any contextual information. I believe, on the contrary, that we cannot understand the relation between a linguistic expression and a real-world situation to which it refers unless we recognize the mediating roles played by the speaker and by the context of the speech event.

In the next chapter we will discuss the notion of autonomous text, attempting to show that it is not a satisfactory approximation of the true relations between linguistic expressions and real-world situations. We will then go on to consider what kinds of constraints are actually imposed upon the choice of linguistic expressions to represent real-world situations. The conclusion will be that those constraints are much looser and more contiguent upon other considerations than the mapping-view of semantics as a matter of truth conditions would allow for.

This chapter will be concerned with how the first question — What is the nature of the 'thing' which we say when we say something? — is to be answered in the reality-construction view of language. We will approach this question through the somewhat broader one: What, in general, is involved in saying something?

It may be surprising, but it is nevertheless true that one of the things concerning language about which we know very little is what is involved in saying something. Since the ability to say things is one of the most valuable advantages conferred on the human species by language, and since we are alone in all the universe — as far as is known — in having this ability, one might have expected that we would have been particularly fascinated by it.

However, it is probably difficult for human beings to see anything mysterious in this ability just because it is so much a part of our everyday experience. And it is not one of the things which the conventional wisdom holds to be mysterious. In any case, if we are to be able to discuss what it is to say the *same* thing, it seems necessary to begin by considering what it is to say a thing at all.

Sentence-level Linguistic Signs

In this chapter and the two which follow it we will be concerned with language in use — that is, linguistic expressions serving as the vehicles of speech acts. However, we will generally not be concerned with the speech act as a whole, but only with its linguistic vehicle. The reason for this is that it is with the linguistic vehicle alone that the intertranslatability postulate is concerned.

The sentence is the linguistic unit whose function it is to serve as the vehicle of speech acts. That is not intended to imply that there are no speech acts whose linguistic vehicles somehow fail to qualify as sentences. Such acts occur frequently, of course. Nor does it imply that speech acts are always, or even typically, limited to a single sentence each. Some acts involve elaborate plans which encompass dozens, hundreds, or even thousands of sentences. Nevertheless, I believe that nothing is lost if we think of the sentence as the representative linguistic sign in speech acts. It will be sufficient to remember that the relevant context in which the sentence is to be used may include other sentences, and among these there may be other sentences which were deliberately put there to serve as a context for the sentence in question.

It is useful to consider sentences to be linguistic signs. As we will see in a later chapter, linguistic signs may be grouped into different categories according to three basic distinctions: (1) sentence-level vs. word-level signs, (2) *ad hoc* vs. conventional signs, and (3) motivated vs. unmotivated signs. Sentences are sentence-level, are always motivated, and are characteristically (although not invariably) *ad hoc* signs.

In what follows, therefore, unless there is some indication to the contrary, a 'linguistic expression' can be thought of as consisting typically of one sentence.

Reality Construction

I do not see any way to talk about what is involved in saying something without immediately recognizing that reality construction is a key part of the process.

It is true that under certain nearly ideal conditions, as when one is reporting a commonplace event which one has witnessed to someone who is of the same cultural background as oneself, the form of the report may seem to be almost automatic. That is, it may seem that virtually all of the details of the report are dictated by the nature of the event. One simply 'tells it like it is'. But note that two conditions were specified: that the event was a commonplace one and that the cultural backgrounds of the speaker and addressee were alike.

It is to be expected that within a particular cultural tradition there will be conventional ways of looking at things which are commonplace within that tradition and conventional ways of talking about them. However, when no such conventional way of looking and talking is available, reporting what happened is likely to demand greater creativity on the part of the reporter. If the event is sufficiently unusual, the speaker may have a great deal of difficulty figuring out what to say about it — what he/she should say it was that happened. (A somewhat similar situation might arise if the addressee was not of the same cultural background. Then, the speaker might find that his/her simple straightforward account was not as readily understandable as he/she might have expected, and it might take some time and effort to straighten out the misunderstandings.)

The problem of reporting an unfamiliar situation can be illustrated with an experiment, designed to illustrate precisely this problem, which I carried out several years ago with a freshman linguistics class.

In this experiment a portion of the class were instructed to imagine that they were beings from a distant world who were viewing our classroom on a television screen. The images were being transmitted by a television camera which had been placed in the classroom at random by a space probe. The beings had had no previous knowledge of anything about any world other than their own. Most importantly, the beings themselves were sentient trees who communicated by telepathy and had created a technology by psychokinesis. They had no knowledge of any beings capable of spontaneous movement. The students were instructed to write *from the perspective of these beings* a brief description of what they saw.[1]

The experiment was designed to have the students assume the role of beings who had no conventional way of looking at (and talking about) the scene with which they were confronted, and to have them then attempt to report what they saw. They all recognized that the task consisted in large part of recognizing the assumptions of their own conventional ways of looking at such things and suppressing any of these assumptions which could be presumed to be inappropriate for the sentient trees whose perspectives they were assuming.

What were the results? Of course, each response differed substantially from each other one, but none of the students succeeded

in freeing him/herself from his/her own habitual way of looking at
the world to the extent that the situation described was designed to
require. For example, all of them somehow found the people in the
room to be that part of the scene which was most deserving of
attention, although the sentient trees who were supposed to be
making the observations should have had no reason to single them
out. In fact, a tree might have been expected to feel a more spontaneous identification with the wooden chairs in the room. Moreover, even though everyone remained seated during the period of
observation, some students were somehow able to distinguish the
persons from the chairs in which they were sitting and even to
report that the normal posture of the persons was one in which
they were straight and vertically oriented. Several observers
inferred that the motions that the students made in writing were
deliberate, even though these observers were totally unacquainted
with the phenomenon of motility. Some observers even commented upon ethnic, sex, and age differences among the persons
under observation. It was apparent that none of the students
succeeded in suppressing all of the assumptions which would have
been relevant to reporting the particular scene under 'normal'
conditions.

The point which this is intended to illustrate is that the representation of reality in language involves far more than a relation of
near isomorphism between the reality and the code. In fact, there
are a number of different steps which we must take to go from
reality (or, more exactly, from the sensory data which constitute
our only information about reality) to linguistic representation.
For example:

(1) We cannot deal with the whole of reality at once; some more
limited segment of it — some excerpt from it — must be singled
out. The assignment given to my students, simply to report
what they could see, although perhaps an unusually open-ended
one, still was focused on a narrow segment of reality in place
and time. And each of the students' reports necessarily analyzed
that segment into smaller aspects.
(2) Even in such a narrowly confined segment of reality, it is
impossible to report everything which presents itself to one's
senses. One decides what is of interest and what is not and on
the basis of that decision leaves entirely out of the account much
of the actual array of sensory impressions.
(3) One perceives relations in what has been singled out to be

reported, i.e. one makes sense of it. For example, imagine a scene which contains among other things (a) a dog running hard and making abrupt sharp turns as it runs, (b) a squirrel sitting on the branch of a tree, (c) a bird flying overhead, (d) a cat somewhat in front of the dog running hard and making abrupt sharp turns which correspond approximately in timing and direction to the turns the dog is making. It would not be surprising if a human observer in such a case inferred that there was a relation between the actions of the dog and those of the cat, attributed purposes to both (the cat having the purpose of escaping the dog; the dog having the purpose of catching the cat), and reported (a) and (d) as a single unit: a dog chasing a cat. In fact, it would be more surprising if he/she did not do so.

In sum, it is quite misleading to speak of the representation of reality as though linguistic utterances were about reality directly.

The linguistic construction of reality may be thought of as occurring on two levels. A language as a whole may be spoken of as reflecting a particular constructed reality. Such realities will be called *Conceptual Worlds*, and will be discussed in more detail in a later chapter. (Actually, since different speakers or different subsets of speakers of a language probably have different linguistic repertoires, it would be more accurate to attribute conceptual worlds to linguistic repertoires rather than to languages. However, it is difficult to escape the standard view of language and its way of talking. Discussion becomes very labored if we resist its implications at every point, or even only at every point where we find them misleading. The fact is, to talk and think in terms of properties of languages rather than properties of repertoires gives the impression of being much simpler and more straightforward. Since this does not seem an appropriate place to contest that issue, we may continue to speak in terms of languages for the moment.)

On a quite different level a single speech act, or rather the linguistic expression which serves as the vehicle of a speech act, also reflects a constructed reality. The constructed realities represented by sentence-level signs will be referred to as *Conceptual Events*. (As was pointed out above, the sentence was chosen because it is the unit designed as the vehicle of speech acts). Here, we will continue the discussion of reality construction on the level of the sentence.

Conceptual Events

Let us take as an example the following sentence: 'A man sold the doctor a car', and let us consider it to have been produced as the report of a simple event (that is, we will suppose that there has been a speech act in which the sentence in question was actually uttered, and uttered appropriately, i.e. it fitted the facts (the next chapter will discuss what it means for a linguistic expression to 'fit the facts')).

Now, although we referred to that expression in such a speech act as the report of a simple event, we should be aware from the outset that what is being reported might not necessarily have been a unitary event from any strictly objective standpoint. It would be perfectly correct to use the sentence in question even if the discussions between the seller and buyer had occurred intermittently over a considerable period of time and even if each participant had been occupied with many unrelated activities during the period of negotiations. It is a single 'event' because the speaker has attributed unity to it — has abstracted certain happenings out of a possibly very extensive context and represented them as constituting a unity. In short, the unity, and therefore the event as an event, is in the eye of the beholder; what constitutes an event is whatever a speaker is able to interpret as one.

Now, an event as represented in a human language is a *structured* unity. It typically consists of a verb and noun phrases or pronouns representing entities of some sort, each with its own designated role. For example, in our sample sentence ('a man sold the doctor a car') the event consists of an act (of the kind called 'selling') which was performed by an 'agent' (of the kind called 'man') and undergone by an 'undergoer' or 'patient' (of the kind called 'car') directed toward what we may call a 'goal' or a 'referent' (of the kind called 'doctor'). What has been done by the speaker actually is to characterize the event which he/she has abstracted as a particular *kind* of event, in which a particular kind of act (selling) has been performed by a particular kind of agent (a man) on a particular kind of patient (a car), etc. Therefore, not only the unity of the event, but also its structure, is in the eye of the beholder — in this case, the speaker.

We may note that what is objectively the same event could have been characterized in different ways by various modifications in the form of the expression. For example, the agent of the hypothetical event might have been characterized differently, e.g. as 'a stooped old man', as 'an Irishman', as 'a school teacher', or any of an infinite number of other possibilities. But note that each of these would have slightly changed the characterization of the event itself, would have characterized it as a slightly different *kind* of event.

But that is only the beginning. The car might have been characterized as 'a 1981 Chevy' or as 'an old wreck', etc.; the doctor might have been characterized in various ways, e.g. as a 'sucker'; the act itself might have been characterized as 'talking (him) into buying', 'unloading (the car on him)', etc. Or the whole event could have been represented in reversed orientation as the doctor (now assigned the role of agent) *buying* the car from a man (now playing a role which we may call 'source').

The point which stands out from this discussion is that it is the speaker who chooses what *kind* of event he/she will represent it as being. The choice is not dictated (except in a quite general way — I will talk more about this in the next chapter) by what actually happened. However, it is limited, of course, by what I will call the 'conceptual elements' of the language, that is, by the kinds of acts and objects and individuals which the particular language recognizes (i.e. has words for).

I like to call such a kind of event a *conceptual event* because the event, as an event, is actually a conception of the speaker. It is the speaker who, first of all, identifies the parts of the event which he/she reports as together constituting a single unity and, secondly, decides how to characterize the structure of the event (in this case an act performed by someone, directed to someone, undergone by something) and its various elements (selling as the act, a man, the doctor, a car, respectively, in the other roles).

Any given language implicitly recognizes, by means of the lexical and grammatical resources which it makes available, an inventory of possible conceptual events. In the hypothetical speech act which we have been discussing (that is, someone saying, 'a man sold the doctor a car' to report an actual event), we may think of the speaker as having selected one conceptual event from that language's inventory of possible conceptual events.

Now, the literature of theoretical linguistics has given great prominence to the fact that the number of potential sentences in any language is infinitely large. Therefore, anyone familiar with that literature may be tempted to object that the inventory of conceptual events provided by any language is actually infinite in size, and that it must consequently be misleading to speak of selecting from an inventory. However, in attempting to translate from one language to another one often finds that the conceptual event specified in the expression to be translated cannot be matched in the target language. The latter's inventory of conceptual events contains nothing comparable. In such circumstances one can be made keenly aware that each language has a limited choice of conceptual events.

Although it is true that, in the final analysis, the inventory of conceptual events of a language is infinitely expandable, it is expandable in one way only and it is not true that all of the infinite inventory is available in the same sense. In fact, the infinite expandability comes about because one can add modifiers to simple structures of the sort we have been discussing. Sentences with complex series of modifiers are not in any realistic sense part of the inventory which an intended speaker initially considers.[2]

In talking about conceptual events we are talking about what seems to be the most important component of the content of a linguistic expression. Although the ability to say things depends upon other factors — other components of content — as well, it is this component which makes it possible to say an infinite number of *different* things. There are two other components of the content of a linguistic expression which I want to talk about. But before doing that I need to say something more about this particularly significant component.

Further Remarks about Conceptual Events

First, there is a problem about terminology. The term 'conceptual event' is being used to refer to a reality model of sentence size. That is, the conceptual event is a key component of the content of a sentence-sized linguistic expression. One reason that the word 'event' is attractive is that it suggests a piece of reality of the right size. Terms such as 'conceptual reality', 'constructed reality', or 'reality model' would be all right except that they might suggest a larger piece of reality, in fact, anything up to a whole world view (what is here being called a 'conceptual world').

However, although 'event' is a good choice in that it suggests units of the right size, it is not really broad enough in meaning to encompass all of the reality models which are being called 'conceptual events' here. For example, it does not seem comfortably to fit the content of sentences such as 'John's sick', or 'Your shoes are under the bed.' One would feel more comfortable referring to these sentences as specifying conceptual 'states of affairs' or 'situations'. In fact, it seems that in those cases where 'event' does not work, 'situation' would do so quite satisfactorily. Thus, we might choose to speak of 'conceptual events *or* situations'. However, that seems to be too clumsy a designation, and therefore it seems best to stick to the simple 'conceptual event', bearing in mind that it is a shorthand label for some such formula as 'conceptual event or situation, etc.'

Secondly, the reader should not be left with the impression that all conceptual events are derivable by simple abstraction from some directly observable reality. Some sentences specify conceptual events (or situations) of such a kind that it is difficult to imagine what kind of direct observations they might be abstracted from. Examples would be 'He forgot to bring any money' or 'She would not condone that sort of thing.' It is hard to imagine how one might observe someone forgetting to bring money (and know that that is what one was observing) or someone being incapable of (or disinclined to, or whatever would be an appropriate condition to observe) condoning some particular sort of thing. In fact, investigation would probably reveal that for a large majority of the conceptual events which occur in ordinary conversation, it would be impossible to imagine direct observations which could confirm their accuracy.

Now it is precisely by means of the specification of the conceptual event that languages (or their users) may be said to construct 'realities'. As should now be apparent, this reality construction plays a key role in our ability (language's ability) to say things. However, a conceptual event does not say anything by itself, nor is it even *about* anything. All that this component of the content does is provide us with an abstract model and, as it were, leave it floating in space. It characterizes an event or situation, but gives no indication as to what context that event or situation is supposed to be relevant to. The second aspect which I want to take up is that which tells us where it fits in.

Contextualization

It is in this aspect that the sayer specifies what he/she is talking about. Often this involves making it clear who is being talked about (who is being 'referred to'). We may illustrate with the sentence which was being used as an example above, viz. 'A man sold the doctor a car.' The conceptual event is, of course, an abstraction. It is a characterization of a *kind* of event — an event of the kind where something which qualifies as selling is performed by something which qualifies as a man, to something which qualifies as a doctor, with the selling undergone by something which qualifies as a car.

But this particular conceptual event is just an abstract characterization very much like an uninterpreted mathematical model. It is an instrument which is available to be used for saying something, but the conceptual event, in itself, does not say anything and is not about anything. Moreover, it cannot be said by itself; the second component of meaning is required to make it sayable.

To return to the example sentence, it has one feature which does not contribute to the specification of the conceptual event, but rather serves to indicate what, or more specifically in this case, who, is being talked about. This is the definite article, 'the', preceding 'doctor'. The 'the' tells the members of the audience that (the speaker thinks that) they know something which should make it possible for them immediately to infer the identity of the buyer. (Since we are supposing that an actual speaker actually said this sentence, in an actual context, to an actual audience, we should assume that that speaker thought that, given what the audience could be presumed to know, the sentence with these hints contained enough information to permit the audience to infer what the sentence was referring to. One would presume that he/she would not have used this particular sentence otherwise.)

What is involved in this final specification is the establishment of — or at least the indication of — a connection between the abstract conceptual event and something within the ken of the intended audience. That is, the use of devices such as the definite article in the example sentence indicates a connection between the abstract model which is the conceptual event and some intended context. Accordingly, we may refer to this aspect of the overall act of saying something as its *contextualization*.

(As I will also briefly indicate in a later chapter, I believe that contextualization (when it does not refer to the speech event itself) will ultimately turn out to consist of placing the conceptual event within what may be thought of as an ongoing discourse. In this conception the available ongoing discourse have a wide range of different relations to the participants in the immediate speech event. One such discourse might be a conversation of which the speech act in question is a part. Others might hark back much further in time or might involve the present speaker and hearer much less directly. This question is not a matter of immediate concern here, so I will not pursue it further. However, I do believe that contextualization will ultimately turn out to be within a discourse rather than within the real world.)

Modality

But there is still a third component to the content of a sentence. Although our sample sentence contains this third component, it is possible to convert the same sentence into a linguistic expression which retains the same conceptual event and the same contextualization but which lacks the third component. For example, we nominalize the sentence to yield the clause, 'the selling of a car to the doctor by a man'. That clause as it is cannot be used to *say* anything, since it lacks the third content component of which we spoke.

One reason why the third component is often overlooked is that we sometimes have a tendency to equate saying with asserting. For example, in *Principia mathematica*, one of the classical works in symbolic logic, Alfred North Whitehead and Bertrand Russell used an 'assertion-sign' (a vertical bar with a horizontal bar projecting to the right from its midpoint). In their words, 'It is required for distinguishing a complete proposition, which we assert, from any subordinate proposition contained in it but not asserted.'[3]

But there are two further distinctions to be made here. First, there are modes of saying other than asserting. To assert is to claim the existence in the envisaged context of an instance of the conceptual event specified in the linguistic expression. For example to assert that (to revert to our example) 'A man sold the doctor a car' is to claim that an event of the kind specified (i.e. the conceptual event) occurred (i.e. was instantiated) in relation to the presumably identifiable doctor (probably within an understood frame of time and place, i.e. in the envisaged context).

But there are other conditions of instantiation which might be specified. For example, an interrogative condition ('Did a man sell the doctor a car?'), a negative one ('didn't sell'), contingent ones of various sorts ('will sell if . . .', 'would have sold if . . .'), ('may have sold', 'may yet sell'), and so on. We may refer to the

component of the content of the linguistic expression which specifies the condition of instantiation as the *modality* component.

The second distinction which we must make is between saying a
particular thing, which is what a speaker sometimes does, and
being used — or being well-designed to be used — by someone to
say that thing, which is what a linguistic expression does. A
linguistic expression does not of itself say anything. It specifies a
conceptual event, it specifies a condition of instantiation for that
event, and it provides some clues as to what context that instantiation of that event is to be placed in, but it does not say anything.
Nothing is said until a speaker, whom we may refer to as a *sayer*[4] in
this capacity, assumes responsibility for the specified condition of
instantiation (of that event in that context).

The conceptual event plus the contextualization clues plus the
modality constitute the content of the linguistic expression. This
content, comprising as it does all three components, constitutes all
of the linguistic paraphernalia which are necessary for saying
something. The issuance of that linguistic expression under the
responsibility of the sayer is what constitutes saying something.

Summary

It was noted that the question of intertranslatability — of how and
to what extent it is possible — is a crucial one for understanding
what kind of thing human language is. We saw, however, that in
order to examine that question closely it would be necessary first to
determine what actually constitutes the content of a linguistic
expression, and, having determined that, then to determine under
what conditions the contents of two different expressions are to be
judged to be the same. This chapter was concerned with the first of
these questions: the nature of the content of a linguistic expression.

An examination of the account of meaning provided by the
mapping view of language showed it to be entirely inadequate, and
we turned to an examination of what actually is involved in saying
something. It was concluded that the construction of realities has a
central role in the saying of anything. It was noted further that the
linguistic construction of reality is actually observable at two
levels. These are the rather fixed constructed reality represented
by a language as a whole and the *ad hoc* reality constructed as part
of an individual speech act — as part of the process of saying something. It is with the latter that we have been concerned in this
chapter.

However, constructed realities do not constitute the whole of the content of a linguistic expression such as a sentence.

In this chapter we have distinguished three components in the content of a sentence. One of these consists of the specification of an abstract event or situation. This was called the *specification of the conceptual event*. The second consists of indications as to how this conceptual event is connected to some thing or things within the ken of the intended audience — how it fits into some ongoing discourse. This was called the *contextualization*. The third component consists of a specification on the authority of the sayer of the condition of instantiation of the conceptual event in the envisaged context (wherein it is asserted, questioned, denied, etc.). This was called the *modality*.

The *saying* is the issuance of the linguistic expression under the authorization of a sayer who thereby assumes responsibility for its content.

Of the three components of the content, it is the conceptual event which will be of greatest interest in the rest of the book. It is this component which shows the greatest variation from language to language. It is this component which plays the key role in the (attempted) use of language to store information; it represents the potential structures of what we call 'facts'. It presents the critical problems for translation of expository text (*per contra*, it does not seem to matter much, for example, whether providing clues as to contextualization is accomplished in the same way in the different languages). And it is, of course, this component in which the linguistic construction of reality is manifested.[5]

Notes

1. In the classroom experiment which I mentioned in the text, the actual instructions were as follows (in fact, the class was divided into three groups, each of which received somewhat different instructions. The first three paragraphs went to all three groups, the fourth paragraph to two, and the final paragraph only to the one group which I am discussing):

'1) Assume that you are watching a television screen. What you see on the screen is the interior of a room in which there is a hidden camera. That room is, in fact, this classroom at this moment.
'2) You are to assume that you have no acquaintance with this room; of course, therefore, you do not recognize it or the people in it.
'3) Your assignment is to write a brief report in which you attempt simply to describe what sort of place you are looking at and what seems to be going on.

'4) You live in a far distant world. Your technology is so advanced that you have been able to transmit the television camera through space and situate it on earth. However, it is the first camera that has been sent to another world, and its winding up in this room is due entirely to chance. Therefore, what you are seeing through the TV set is your first view of another world.

'5) Further background: You are a large tree on a world which does not have any animal life. Although your species has no ability to move, it does have highly developed extra-sensory perception. Your powers of psychokinesis (the ability to control the movements of external objects by means of the mind) are so advanced that you have created a complex technology based on making tools move in precisely controlled ways. You communicate by telepathy with one another. Keep these facts in mind in writing your report'.

2. My assertion that sentences with complex series of modifiers are not in any realistic sense part of the inventory which an intended speaker initially considers is based in large part on the careful research of Frances Hodgetts Syder and Andrew Pawley on spoken language (cf. Syder 1983, Pawley and Syder 1983a, b).

3. The quotation from *Principia mathematica* is taken from page 8 of Whitehead and Russell 1957 (a reprinting of the second edition which was originally published in 1925).

4. As regards my function of 'sayer', I should point out that Ervin Goffman (1981: 144 and *passim*) makes further distinctions of roles. He distinguishes the 'animator' who produces the actual sounds, the 'author' who selected the sentiments expressed and the wording used, and the 'principal' who believes in or is at least committed to what the words say. These distinctions all seem valid, although they are apparently not necessary for my present purposes.

5. One final point is worth mentioning here. I understand the object of the study known as 'semantics' to be the content of linguistic expressions — i.e. of the vehicles of speech acts (real or potential). That is what this chapter was about. However, this object of study is often called 'referential meaning' (to distinguish it from 'social meaning' or the total meaning conveyed by a speech act in context, etc.). The term referential meaning seems particularly unfortunate in the light of what has been said here because it seems to commit the field of semantics irrevocably to the mapping view of language. Surely, it would be preferable to use a less loaded term, perhaps 'representational meaning', to distinguish the object of semantics from other things which may be referred to as meaning. I am convinced that even those who seek to divert attention from the study of language as such to that of language use have much to gain in the long run from a more realistically conceived semantics.

4

Conceptual Events and Real-world Situations

The last chapter was concerned with determining how the content of linguistic expressions such as sentences is to be characterized in the reality-construction view of language. The question which it attempted to answer was: what kind of thing is a thing which we say — what is a 'sayable thing'? The answer was that there are at least three distinguishable components in the content of a linguistic expression, but that we could devote most of our attention to one of these. The key component is the conceptual event.

The question which we are still left with in this chapter and the next is: on what basis are we to say that sayable things are 'the same'? In seeking to answer this question we will focus on the conceptual events of the different linguistic expressions.

The last chapter gave a sketch which was intended to show how these two questions are answered in the mapping view of language. The mapping-view answer to the second question was that two linguistic expressions say the same thing if the set of real-world situations to which each may truly refer is the same.

I suggested that the most serious error in that view of language was that it sees the relation between linguistic expressions and real-world situations as an immediate one. That is, it attributes to the linguistic expressions the qualities of autonomous text which so precisely specifies its own meaning that it is completely understandable without reference to any contextual information. It was pointed out there that we cannot understand the relationship between a linguistic expression and a real-world situation to which it refers unless we recognize the mediating roles played by the speaker and by the context of a speech event.

This chapter will seek to clarify those points. First, it will

41

consider the concept of autonomous text, and explain how the relation which it posits between the linguistic expression and the real world is alien to the nature of language. Then, we will consider the relations which in ordinary language use are actually expected to obtain between linguistic expressions, or more specifically, conceptual events, and real-world situations.

Against the Notion of Autonomous Text

The term 'autonomous text' refers to linguistic expressions whose content is encoded so completely and unambiguously into the expression that it will be forever available without distortion to anyone who approaches that expression with the necessary knowledge of language, i.e. with the only requisite knowledge being narrowly linguistic in nature. We may begin with the stipulation that constructing autonomous text is obviously not the main function of human language; that it is not what language was designed to do. Or to put it more accurately, the selective pressures to which the evolution of language is a response could not have included the construction of autonomous text, if for no other reason than that autonomous text is surely dependent upon the existence of writing.

Furthermore, an instrument for producing truly autonomous text in the sense intended would have to be a well-defined system; that is, all of its possible signata would have to be specified precisely. This specification might be achieved by means of rigorously formulated syntactic rules and a fixed vocabulary whose signata were precisely defined in terms of the external world. However, natural languages are not such well-defined systems.

It seems obvious that the view of language in which autonomous text can even be conceived of is the result of efforts to use language as an instrument for certain purposes. These efforts have led to a view of language in which it appears to have many of the characteristics which would be necessary in an instrument suitable for those purposes. For example, I believe that we can describe the role which philosophers of science have traditionally expected language to play as that of fixing units of information and encoding them in autonomous text for the purpose of transmitting or storing them. This hypothetical language of autonomous text is the language of the unified science envisaged by the positivists and that of the 'information society' which is said to be looming over the horizon.

Although it seems obvious enough that this view of language is a relatively recent invention, that is not in itself a sufficiently strong argument to cause it to be abandoned. On the contrary, the assumption that languages are, or may reasonably be thought of as if they were, instruments for producing autonomous text might be supported by an argument of what can be called the *close-enough* type. What I mean by a 'close-enough-type' argument is an argument that a particular model (or 'view') of a certain subject matter is justified because, even though it has not been possible to make the actual observations of the subject matter fit the model, some approximation to a fit has been achieved. Such an argument with respect to the concept of autonomous text might proceed along something like the following lines:

'While it is admittedly true that we cannot as yet specify in detail exactly how language can be used to produce autonomous text, working out those details is precisely the main problem that our science is concerned with. Moreover, even supposing that matters are worse yet, and that completely autonomous text is not possible at all, that still is no serious problem. It is no serious problem because it is not necessary for our view of the nature of language to be absolutely correct in all of its details. All that matters — at this stage of research, in any case — is that we know what *kind* of thing language is. And since, surely, our experience shows that we can make some kind of approximation to autonomous text in the sense intended, whatever flaws there may be in our view of the nature of language may be regarded as matters of detail. Although an error of *kind* in our conception of the nature of language would be cause for concern, uncertainty and even erroneous assumptions about details are not. In fact, they are to be expected, and there will be plenty of time to deal with them when our detailed knowledge reaches the point that we can specify what they are'.

So might the argument go.

The key point in this argument is that we are in fact able to produce a fairly close approximation to autonomous text. In order to show the weakness of the argument, we need to consider what that approximation consists of.

It seems clear that in the final analysis all that we are able to accomplish by way of approximating autonomous text is simply to anticipate as best we can the kinds of contexts in which the text might be read. That is, we attempt to anticipate what kinds of audiences there might be, what kinds of background they might have, under what circumstances they might be reading what is being written, what purposes they might attribute to the writer, etc. On the basis of all of these imagined contextualizations we attempt to anticipate how each type of person envisaged might go about making sense of what has been drafted, and then we attempt to revise the draft so as to forestall any of those interpretations which are undesirable. In other words, we do not produce prose which is independent of context; rather, we attempt to foresee the possible contextualizations and to allow for them.

It must, in fact, be extremely unusual for anyone to attempt to write anything with the intention of making it understandable to literally everyone. Indeed, it is certainly the case that the kind of text which most closely approaches the ideal of autonomousness is expository text designed for a culturally very narrowly conditioned audience limited to individuals who have been shaped by a particular kind of educational tradition which is an integral part of Western Civilization. In most cases the intended audience will all have shared a very specialized professional training. All that a text can actually do, then, in the way of having a well-defined meaning for any readers is to have that meaning for just those readers who meet certain requirements and who are reading under conditions which meet certain requirements.

I would maintain, therefore, that a view of language in which it is seen as an instrument for producing autonomous text does not come close enough to the actual nature of language for any practical purposes *except* for one particular mission. This mission is to produce a theory of language design suitable for applications in the formulation of scientific statements and in encoding and performing operations upon 'information'.

Real-world Situation and Linguistic Expression

We have said that the mapping view of language, with its notion of autonomous text, misrepresents the relation between linguistic expressions and real-world situations to which they refer. The mapping view and, especially, the notion of truth conditions give particular prominence to the constraints imposed upon the design of linguistic expressions by real-world situations to which they refer. It will be seen that this relation appears in a quite different light in the reality-construction view of language.

The point which requires clarification, then, concerns the relation which exists between the linguistically constructed realities

44

and actual reality. In the mapping view, the meaning of a linguistic expression is defined as the set of conditions under which it would be true (I will refer to the concept of meaning represented by this definition as 'truth-conditional semantics'). The truthfulness of a statement is therefore to be determined by confronting the statement with appropriate observations of the real world to determine whether conditions under which it would be true actually obtain.

But if we reject this mapping view, is there even such a thing as truth or falsity? It will be better to approach this question via a still more general one: On what basis is it that we can say that some statements are right and others wrong? In short, what relation, if any, do we require a conceptual event to show to actual fact?

On Confronting a Conceptual Event with the Facts

Consider an example. We see a dog bite a man, and I say, 'I will propose a description of what we just saw. The description is, "A dog bit a man." Is that statement true?'

And you all agree that it is true. Then someone proposes another description of the same event. It is: 'A man bit a dog.' And everyone agrees that that statement is false. That is exactly what truth-conditional semantics would predict. If this book wishes to maintain that truth-conditional semantics misrepresents the way in which ordinary language works, how does it account for the case in point? Or, to state the question more generally, how *are* the conceptual realities represented by language related to actual reality?

There are several points related to that question that need to be clarified before an answer can be attempted. First, the question as stated could be interpreted as asking about the way in which the repertoire of elements of the language as a whole represents reality as a whole. That is an interesting question in its own right and one which will be discussed later in the book. However, the immediate question concerns the appropriate use of conceptual *events* to represent actual events (or at least to represent some segment of actuality).

Secondly, some linguistic expressions do not even purport to represent any actual reality. Works of fiction are examples of these. There is no actual reality with which they can be confronted. (Note that the requirement of verisimilitude for a work of

45

fiction to be successful, whatever its precise nature, is an entirely different matter from that under discussion).

Thirdly, some statements, even though they do purport to represent actual realities, represent realities which could not easily be brought into confrontation with them. Consider these examples: 'All birds have feathers' or 'The polarity of the earth's magnetic field has been reversed several times during the life of the earth.' In such cases the appropriate facts about actual reality might be somewhat more difficult to ascertain even though in each case actual physical reality is involved. But that is not the worst of it. Consider this:

In the case of many sentences which appear to be intended as statements of fact, it is hard to imagine what kind of observable reality they should be thought of as purporting to fit.

That sentence is my own, and I used it here because I wanted to say what it says. But it also serves to illustrate the kind of sentence that it refers to. How would one go about establishing whether or not it is in fact true that 'in the case of many sentences which appear to be intended as statements of fact, it is hard to imagine what kind of observable reality they should be thought of as purporting to fit'? What observable facts do we consult to determine what something 'purports to fit', what 'should be thought' about anything, or whether something 'is hard to imagine'?

However, none of these problems are relevant to the real question being asked here. The difficulty which they present is difficulty in ascertaining the exact nature of the actual reality involved. That hardly seems to have anything to do with the nature of language. However, the mapping view of language would perhaps not have given us much reason to expect this difficulty to occur, while the reality-constuction view would perhaps have left us better prepared to expect it. Anyway, what we need to discuss here is how we judge the adequacy of the relationship of linguistic representations to actual realities when all of the facts are available to us.

Designing a Conceptual Event

Let us begin by considering how the process of cummunication by language works. As was explained elsewhere, when one says something, one specifies a conceptual event. One puts forward a model of an event, and the model is made up of conceptual elements.

Conceptual elements have not been discussed yet in this book. It will suffice for the moment to say that the elements (or concepts) are known to speakers of the language as something like stereotypes. That is, they each have some kind of mental picture (except that the word 'picture' suggests something too explicitly visual) of a particular *kind* of object, act, etc. Whatever else they might involve, these stereotypes would involve some idea of what significance the presence of that particular element in a situation might have for the speaker in question. For example, my own stereotype of 'snake' would emphatically not be just some notions about how to recognize a snake: it would also include a strong conscious awareness that some snakes are dangerous and also, probably, a general aversion.

I must admit to being still very vague on the nature of stereotypes. I described them as 'mental pictures', but then pointed out that that characterization suggests something too explicitly visual. What I would like to suggest is that they are somehow derived from our experiences with the element in question. If the element is a kind of physical reality which we have often seen, then our mental picture is likely to have a visual aspect. On the other hand, elements such as the 'Holy Ghost', 'idea', 'to introspect', or the like, may not have any visual aspect at all. For the present I can only suggest that our stereotype for a particular element somehow reflects the conditions that have been associated with the presence of the element in our experience.

To continue the account of the process of communication by language, suppose that I have specified a conceptual event. Now you, as a speaker of the same language, share approximately the same elements. That is, each sign corresponds to a stereotype for you as well, and in most cases our stereotypes will be quite similar. It is a reasonable expectation that they will be similar, since speakers of the same language will usually have acquired their stereotypes in roughly the same ways and in response to similar influences. In any case, the use of language to communicate is based on the assumption that the stereotypes of speaker and audience are equivalent.

You, then, on hearing what I say, imagine (in some sense of the word) an event of the kind which I have characterized — of the kind that my model represents. You, of course, make use of your own stereotypes, but we have agreed that they are likely to be reasonably similar to mine. When I say that you imagine it, recall that that does not necessarily imply a visual image, but in some form you have this kind of event in mind. (I am, of course, assuming that you are paying attention and are making a reasonable effort to understand). In fact, all the evidence of which I am aware suggests that you almost surely will go well *beyond* what I have specified about the event, in fleshing it out — filling in details. A model, after all, represents only the general structure of the event.

If my utterance purports to convey information about some real state of affairs, the question of goodness of fit to that reality comes up. However, not all utterances do so, as we have seen. What we are concerned with is the question of goodness of fit of a verbal model to actual reality in the kind of circumstances which are most favorable for comparing them. Suppose (to continue with our previous example) that someone has said, 'A dog bit a man' and that we had been observing the very place where this was purported to have happened at the time when it was purported to have happened. Thus, we can compare the asserted model (the statement) with the observed reality.

More precisely, each person involved will have his or her own mental image corresponding to the statement, and it is that mental image which will be confronted with the observed reality. Therefore, the judgments of goodness of fit actually concern the fit between mental images and reality (as observed), and it is quite possible for different individuals to arrive at different judgments. However, these different images all purport to correspond to the same verbal representation, and it may be assumed that all will usually correspond fairly closely to one another. Therefore, it seems justifiable to speak of the fit between reality and linguistic representations, and we may continue to discuss the case in point in those terms. We are to compare the asserted model of 'A dog bit a man' to the observed reality. What kinds of criteria do we apply and what kinds of judgments are available to us?

Requirements of Fit between Linguistic Expression and Actual Reality

The following considerations are pertinent:

1) In everyday language use we tend to reserve such concepts as truth and falsehood for the speaker's intentions. A recent study reported by Linda Coleman and Paul Kay confirms this.[1] In their study, subjects were asked to consider statements made in

a number of hypothetical situations and to judge in each case whether or not the statement was a lie. They found that the subjects were most likely to label the statement a lie if the speaker believed it to be false, somewhat less likely to do so if the speaker, although not believing it to be false, had said it with the intent of deceiving his/her audience, and still less likely to do so if neither of these conditions obtained even if the statement was in fact false.

2) Generally, if we think the speaker's intentions are good and that he/she is not clearly mistaken, we are likely to interpret inaccuracy as lack of preciseness rather than as lack of truthfulness. In other words, instead of a sharp line between truth and falsity, there are degrees of *goodness of fit*. We judge in terms of goodness of fit between our stereotypes corresponding to the elements in the model and the observed reality i.e. how closely the thing doing the biting fits our idea of a dog, how closely what it did fits our idea of biting, etc.

3) The degree of goodness of fit called for varies widely from event to event — it varies depending on what the speaker's point is — what the purpose of the utterance is. Sometimes it is convenient to settle for a fairly loose fit.

Linguists have frequently commented on the extent of inexactness in language use. Dwight Bolinger has gone so far as to say, 'It is characteristic of natural language that no word is ever limited to its enumerable senses, but carries within it the qualification of "something like"'.[2] George Lakoff and others have pointed out the frequency with which we resort to what they call 'hedges'.[3] Examples of hedges are 'sort of', 'kind of', 'loosely speaking', 'more or less', 'roughly', 'pretty (much)', 'as it were', 'in a way', 'in a manner of speaking', 'so to speak'.

To illustrate the relevance of the speaker's purpose to determining the requirements of goodness of fit, consider the following hypothetical situation: A is describing to B some event which he (A) has observed. His description includes something done or said by a third party, C. What C did was of relevance to A's story only because it served as a stimulus for what happened next, and A's account of C's behavior is a casual one. It only needs to be accurate enough to advance the story in the intended way.

However, suppose it now turns out that C is well known to B, and that B finds the behavior attributed by A to C (for example, political views expressed) noteworthy. B asks A to confirm that the account was indeed accurate and to provide further details of the context.

Now the situation has suddenly changed. A now has been assigned a different purpose to pursue, one which calls for a quite different fit between C's actual behavior and the account given of it. It is likely that A will find it necessary to pause to reflect, and that he will finally give a significantly different account of C's behavior in the new circumstances.

Note, however, that the first account should not be thought of as having been untruthful. It was just that the concern with producing a good fit between the report — the model — and the actual reality focused upon another part of the model (and of the reality).

4) If a person expends more than a certain amount of time and effort to assure goodness of fit between his/her statements and reality, we may judge him/her to be overly fastidious. On the other hand, if he/she is satisfied with a quite inexact fit, we may judge him/her to be unreliable — his/her reports to be untrustworthy. Therefore, maintaining a balance may demand a considerable amount of attention.

For example, we may note that it is appropriate sometimes to speak 'roughly'. J. L. Austin gave as an example the statement, 'France is hexagonal'. As he pointed out, it is really not appropriate to ask whether that statement is true or false. It is true in a rough sense, but if we choose to be precise about it, it is false. The shape of France is a rough approximation of that of an irregular hexagon, but it is certainty not a mathematically exact one. It all depends on the nature of our interest in the shape of France. In short, the fit between statement and reality is satisfactory for some conceivable purposes and unsatisfactory for others.

Another example of Austin's is 'Oxford is 60 miles from London'. He points out that the goodness of fit required of that statement will normally be less strict than of the statement, 'Oxford is 63.5 miles from London'.[4] If the second statement is found to be inaccurate by one mile, that degree of misfit is likely to be judged more serious than would an inaccuracy of the same amount (i.e. one mile) discovered in the first.

Some Kinds of Misfit

Let us examine briefly some finds of misfit and the considerations involved in judging them. I will once more use the statement, 'A dog bit a man', to provide examples of some kinds of misfit and thereby further to illustrate the complications involved in the question of sufficient goodness of fit.

An experience I once had is illustrative. On that occasion I ventured into the territory guarded by a large dog. The dog threatened and then lunged at me, striking me on the knee with its teeth (or perhaps only a single tooth). It then backed away, ending the episode. It struck me hard enough to produce a bruise, but there was no puncture or abrasion. The incident sticks in my mind because I had some difficulty at the time deciding whether or not I should say that the dog had bitten me, thereby over-simplifying as it seemed to me (since I do not feel that what it did was exactly biting, certainly not a prototypical example of biting). The alternative would have been to give a somewhat more exact but necessarily more lengthy description of what had happened, thereby presuming perhaps unduly upon the patience of my audience.

Suppose, then, that what had taken place between the dog and the man referred to in our statement was the same thing that happened to me. How should we decide in that case, whether or not the goodness of fit of statement to reality is satisfactory?

To take a different example, suppose that the animal which did the biting was not a dog but a pet wolf. Would that inaccuracy be sufficient to make the fit of the statement to the reality unsatisfactory? Again the question cannot be answered in a vacuum. We must take the purpose of the speaker (and perhaps the purposes of the audience as well) into account. For example, if the main concern was the injuries suffered by the victim, then the inaccuracy of attributing the responsibility to a dog would probably not be judged to deserve much weight. However, if the main concern were, for example, to support an argument that dogs were dangerously unpredictable and should be subjected to a more stringent leash law, this particular inaccuracy should presumably be regarded as critical.

Suppose again that the bitten person was a minor, not a man but a boy. Again the speaker's purpose is of crucial importance, but for most purposes, this would probably be regarded as a fairly trivial inexactitude. After all, there is a continuum between childhood and adulthood. However, the weight given to the error might increase in proportion to the youthfulness of the boy.

Suppose, finally, that instead of a man or a boy the victim was a woman disguised as a man. This seems to be a different matter. The statement now seems definitely in error since there is no continuum involved and it is hard to think of 'man' as being only slightly off the mark — as being just the first word that popped into the speaker's mind and one that constituted a close enough approximation (an argument that obviously does work in some cases). However, the speaker seems likely to be held blameless. It is difficult to imagine a purpose which the speaker might have had in uttering this statement which would have obligated him/her to investigate the sex of the victim in sufficient depth to have penetrated a deliberate disguise.

We have been considering hypothetical cases in which it is possible to confront a linguistic characterization of an actual reality with the reality itself and then to consider what factors are involved in determining whether or not the fit of the first to the second is satisfactory. But of course when people talk, it is not usually to tell us what is happening right in front of our eyes. Normally, the verbal expression contributes something that was not otherwise available (else why bother with it at all?).

It seems fairly clear what it contributes in the case of a statement like 'A dog bit a man' (assuming that we have enough information otherwise to determine what the speaker is talking about). It tells us of the existence of a reality which fits the statement reasonably well. Of course, if we have no other knowledge of the event in question, we cannot be sure that the statement is not an error or a deliberate lie. What we have is a mental image, but we think of it as corresponding to a reality which might be encompassed at a glance.

In cases such as the example concerning the earth's polarity we also have a mental image, but most likely without any notion of such a neatly circumscribed and sensorily apprehensible corresponding reality.

The case of fiction is different again. Again we have only the mental image which it evokes. However, here there is no pretence that there is any corresponding actual reality. The corresponding reality is an *as-if* reality. The speaker's (writer's) purpose is clearly different (as is the listener's or reader's), and the linguistic product must be judged accordingly.

Thus, the question of the relation between actual reality and its linguistic representations is a very valid one, and I have tried to show in a very preliminary way what direction an answer to it would need to take. However, I believe that the very partial answer which I have proposed here is sufficient to show why I say that the truth-conditional view of semantics so seriously misrepresents the way in which ordinary language works that we are not likely to learn much (about *ordinary* language) from it.

Conclusions

Perhaps the most important point which emerges from this chapter is that the way in which language works in ordinary use is radically different from that envisaged in the mapping view. Ordinary language use is not concerned with drawing precise boundaries to define the conditions under which a word or a sentence may be correctly used. That is, in fact, an entirely unnatural goal in any but quite exceptional cases. The fact is that the mapping view has its roots in prescriptivism. It never came close to representing the way language works. It represented the way some people thought it ought to be *made* to work.

The mapping view is intimately associated historically with writing, and more specifically with a particular tradition of expository writing.[5] This tradition aimed at producing what has been called 'autonomous text'. Autonomous text would consist of context-free statements — statements which would have a single uniform interpretation in any conceivable context. They would thus be capable of accurately encoding and storing information, which, once encoded and put into storage would remain invariant. Exactly the original information would be retrievable by anyone at any time in the future.

Among the difficulties with this ideal, of course, are its exaggerated conceptions of how close languages come to being universal encoders, how close individual languages come to being well-defined systems, and what is involved in really learning a language. That is not to say that the ideal is not worth pursuing. To achieve the nearest approximation possible to it would seem to be very useful for some, e.g. scientific, purposes. What is so misguided is seeking to see such characteristics in language in general. To do so does not even aid in designing a language for science.

Notes

1. The study on the use of the word 'lie' is Coleman and Kay 1981.
2. The Bolinger quotation is from Bolinger 1965: 567.
3. Lakoff's original work on 'hedges' was Lakoff 1972.
4. Both Austin examples are taken from Austin 1963: 32.
5. My remarks about the strong influence of patterns of language use associated with literacy on our 'mapping' view of language draw on much recent work. Prominent sources have been the work of Frances Hodgetts Syder and Andrew Pawley (cf. Syder 1983, Pawley and Syder 1983a, b), Walter J. Ong (cf. Ong 1982 and many works), and David R. Olson (1977a, b).

5

The Problem of Translation

The intertranslatability postulate, i.e. the assumption that anything which can be said in one language can be said in any other language, was identified as holding the key to the differences between the two views of language which are being examined here. It may be regarded as the very cornerstone of the first of these views, that which we are calling the mapping view, while it is not accepted by the other, the reality-construction view. Both of the last two chapters have been attempts to explicate some of the points of disagreement.

Chapter 3 was concerned with what it means to 'say a thing', or more exactly with determining what kind of thing a thing which is said can be. To put it in still another way, it was concerned with analyzing that which we call the 'meaning' or the 'content' of a linguistic expression such as a sentence. The conclusion, it will be recalled, was that this content has at least three components. They were called, respectively, a 'conceptual event', a 'contextualization', and a 'modality'. A further conclusion was that it was the first of these, the conceptual event, which presented the principal problem in translation, and that it was probably sufficient for our present purposes to focus our attention primarily on it.

We have seen that, according to the mapping view, the meaning of an expression is defined in terms of the real-world situations which it might properly refer to. And, according to the same view, two expressions say the same thing if the real-world situations which they may properly refer to are the same. In the reality-construction view, the relation between linguistic expressions and real-world situations is seen as more complex. As we saw in

Chapter 3, the meaning of a linguistic expression such as a sentence is seen as quite abstract — not directly connected with the conditions which might be employed in classifying real-world situations. In this view, therefore, a linguistic expression cannot, of itself, refer to anything; it is a sayer who refers. Although the linguistic expression is the instrument which the sayer uses in referring, there are no rigid built-in constraints as to what can or cannot be referred to by means of a particular linguistic expression.

However, the reality-construction view does of course recognize that the relation between conceptual events and the real-world situations which they are used to talk about is far from a random one. Therefore, in order to make clearer the differences between the two views, it seemed necessary to discuss how we decide whether or not the use of a particular linguistic expression to refer to a particular real-world situation is proper, and that was the subject of Chapter 4. We found that truth or falsity in the strict sense plays only a limited role, and that much depends upon the speaker's purposes.

In this chapter we will consider from the standpoint of the reality-construction view of language what it means for two linguistic expressions to have the 'same' meaning — to 'say the same thing'. The conclusion will be that there is only one answer which can be formulated with enough clarity to permit it to be used and that that answer forces us to reject the intertranslatability postulate. In fact, that answer suggests that in almost every case where it *is* possible to say the same thing in two different languages that possibility is due to special historical circumstances.

Let us use the term 'translation equivalents' to designate a source-language expression together with a target-language expression which we are considering (at least tentatively) as its translation. As a starting point, we may assume that if a pair of translation equivalents show identical (or approximately identical) conceptual events, (approximately) identical modalities, and provide clues which suggest the same contextualization, the one is in fact a satisfactory translation of the other, i.e. the two do in fact 'say the same thing'. However, as has already been pointed out, it is the conceptual event which poses the greatest problem for translation. Therefore, it seems permissible, and at this stage of investigation expedient, to restrict our attention to the treatment of the conceptual event in translation equivalents. We will thereby tentatively assume that means for adequately representing the other components of the content can always be found.

Let us begin, therefore, by considering translation equivalents in which the target-language expression may be said to preserve the same conceptual event as the source-language expression. A translation may be said to preserve the same conceptual event if the verb of the original expression is translated by the verb of the target-language expression and each of the arguments of the original is translated by an argument in the same case relation in the target-language expression. We may refer to translation equivalents which preserve the same conceptual event as *isomorphic*.[1] Let us begin, therefore, by contrasting isomorphic and non-isomorphic, or 'paraphrastic', translation.

Isomorphic vs. Paraphrastic Translation

Isomorphic translation may be illustrated by the following translation equivalents between English and French. These examples are taken from the book, *Stylistique comparée du français et de l'anglais: Méthode de traduction*, by Jean-Paul Vinay and J. Darbelnet.[2]

1) E: The ink is on the table./F: *L'encre est sur la table.* (Literally: the-ink-is-on-the-table).

2) E: I left my spectacles on the table downstairs./F: *J'ai laissé mes lunettes sur la table en bas.* (Literally: I-(have-)left-my-spectacles-on-the-table-(in-bottom(downstairs))).

3) E: Where are you?/F: *Où êtes vous?* (Literally: where-are-you?).

Now it is important to realize that non-isomorphic translation, i.e. *paraphrastic* translation, is a fundamentally different *kind* of thing from isomorphic translation. There are a number of points of difference. Let us examine three of them:

(1) Isomorphic translation does not, at least in theory, require that the translator understand the original message (however, see the qualification concerning compulsory categories discussed below). In fact, it seems at least theoretically possible that such translation might eventually be performed by machines having at their disposal extensive bilingual dictionaries and syntactic reference materials. It is important to keep in mind, however, that this sort of mechanical translation would be satisfactory only for as long as the isomorphism could be satisfactorily sustained. Paraphrastic translation, on the contrary, requires that the translator

understand what is being said. Understanding something which has been said is a very complicated achievement, and it is one which was received very little attention in the linguistic literature[3] (however, a few limited comments will be devoted to it later in this chapter and in Chapter 10).

Where isomorphic translation is not possible, the translator has no resource but to attempt to understand the speaker's intentions well enough to design an utterance in the target language which is suitable for serving the same intentions. More exactly, what must be understood is what the speaker *gives us* (*the audience*) *to understand* are his/her intentions (the 'authorized inferences' as to his/her intentions). Understanding these intentions may require 'extra-linguistic' knowledge of a number of different kinds. It will also require attention to the context of the speech act — both the linguistic and the extra-linguistic aspects of that context.

The latter consideration underlines a second and third point of difference between isomorphic and paraphrastic translation:

(2) Isomorphic translation can, under favorable conditions, be performed upon a single linguistic expression, such as a sentence, without regard to any context of its use, real or imagined. That is simply not possible for paraphrastic translation (which requires that the translator understand and take into account what is going on).

(3) Isomorphic translation translates each sentence as a separate unit — it is a sentence-by-sentence mapping between the languages. Such translation maintains isomorphism of the conceptual event, and each sentence (except for sentences consisting of more than one clause connected by co-ordinating conjunctions) employs just one conceptual event in *saying* what it says. (Although other conceptual events may be represented in relative clauses, they are not part of what the sayer, strictly speaking, takes responsibility for.) Of course, one can translate longer passages and will often be called upon to do so, but if the standard of translation required is equivalence of the conceptual events, then the problem is simply multiplied by the number of sentences.

In paraphrastic translation it will often not be possible, let alone practical, to match sentence to sentence. Moreover, even when it is possible to translate a particular sentence with a single sentence, the translator may still be obliged to consider the other sentences (as well as everything else) in the context in order to achieve the kind of overall understanding that is required for an adequate translation of the particular sentence in question.

Quasi-isomorphic Translation

The examples of isomorphic translation between English and French which were cited above matched each other almost word for word. Before assuming that the only alternative to such isomorphism is a paraphrastic translation which requires the translator to understand the original message, we should consider whether or not any possibilities exist of devising specific transformations of the original conceptual event which will produce a permissible sequence in the target language and at the same time adhere acceptably closely to the conceptual structure of the source.

As a starting point, we should take note of the fact that there are several ways in which the translation equivalents can depart from the close parallelism of the previous examples and still be counted as isomorphic. For instance:

1) There are two obvious kinds of difference between translation equivalents which are due to grammatical differences between languages. The most trivial probably is difference in word order as dictated by the respective grammars.

2) A second kind of difference which would probably be classed as grammatical by most people consists of differences in what are sometimes called 'compulsory categories'.[4] Compulsory categories are grammatical categories, and thence usually, categories of information which must be included in a sentence of a certain sort. For example, in a broad class of instances in English is it necessary to show grammatically whether a noun is singular or plural. It is impossible in such instances (i.e. where a 'count' noun is involved) to omit the information. (There are means to circumvent this rule if one is determined to do so, but they involve resorting to circumlocutory sentence structures.) Thus, if one is translating into English a sentence which contains nouns of the appropriate class but with no specification of number, the number will have to be supplied in the English translation.

This kind of instance is of particular interest because it marks a departure from the general principle that isomorphic translation does not require the translator to understand the original. Obviously, when one is required to supply compulsory category information which was lacking in the original, one must have some understanding of the original.

Other examples of compulsory categories in English which

often require a translator to supply information from his/her own understanding include gender in pronouns (whether to choose 'he', 'she', or 'it') and tense (present, past, future, etc.) in verbs.

3) Another sort of difference between translation equivalents is what Vinay and Darbelnet call *modulation figée* ('fixed' or 'frozen modulation').[5] What is involved here is a difference in the composition of the words or idioms which serve as translation equivalents in the two languages. Two of Vinay and Darbelnet's favorite examples of fixed modulation are 'fire-boat' and 'fireman' vs. *bateau-pompe* and *pompier*, respectively.

Although such differences have no effect whatever on truth conditions, they are capable of producing quite different effects on the hearer (as witness arguments in American media over the choice between the terms 'pro-lifer' and 'anti-abortionist'). In the terminology which will be presented in the next chapter of this book, such translation equivalents would be said to have like *senses*, but unlike *characterizations*.

Although the translation equivalents in these examples reflect departures from a strict morpheme-for-morpheme mapping, they nevertheless remain within the bounds of isomorphic translation as it is defined here.

It should be noted, however, that it is sometimes possible to produce translation equivalents which depart from isomorphism only in limited and clearly specifiable ways. We might refer to these as *quasi-isomorphic* translation equivalents. What I have in mind here is what Vinay and Darbelnet in the book mentioned above call *transposition*. In transposition, the model of the original language expression is still recognizable, but some elements of the meaning are carried by grammatically different elements in the target language. One of their examples is English 'He limped across the street' vs. French *Il a traversé la rue en boitant*, where the semantic contribution of 'across' corresponds approximately to that of the verb in the French, and *en boitant* makes a semantic contribution corresponding roughly to that of the verb of the English.[6]

It is possible in cases such as the above to think of a content or, more precisely, of a conceptual event which has been transformed in ways which can be exactly specified. That is, the transformations leading from one conceptual event to the other can be traced. It does not seem inconceivable that the necessary transpositions between two particular languages could be specified in such a way that they could be applied automatically, i.e. without the necessity for the translator to understand the meaning of the original linguistic expression. However, I have been able to think of no further kinds of automatic transformations comparable to this. Therefore, it seems that once we pass beyond quasi-isomorphism, we have entered the realm where paraphrastic translation is the only recourse that remains.[7]

Paraphrastic Translation

Consider an example of Whorf's. Whorf cites the Shawnee *nipēkwālakha*, 'I clean it (gun) with a ramrod.' (Although Whorf notes in the parentheses that the object cleaned is intended to be a gun, it seems evident that 'gun' is not part of the original meaning, that is, it is not specified in the expressions cited for either language, and could only be inferred by recourse to contextual information.) The Shawnee expression is analyzed by Whorf as follows: *ni* ('I'), *pēkw* ('dry space'), *ālak* ('interior of hole'), *h* ('by motion of tool, instrument'), *a* ('cause to another').[8]

Now it is clear that there is nothing approaching isomorphism between the Shawnee and English equivalents. It also seems quite apparent that they could not translate each other except in a context where the very specific act of 'cleaning' a gun in the special sense of using a ramrod to move a piece of fabric or the like through the barrel in order to remove foreign matter, especially the residue of charred powder resulting from the firing of the gun, is the subject of discussion.

However, the English sentence itself could actually be used for a wide variety of acts. The sentence is built around the verb 'to clean' which is applicable to any act designed to render any object more 'clean', and what counts as clean or cleaner depends to a considerable extent on the object involved. Thus, 'I clean it with the ramrod' would be appropriate to any situation where what I do to 'it' counts as cleaning and where I somehow make use of the ramrod as an instrument. For example, imagine that I have a small rug placed where it collects a lot of sand from people coming in from the beach. Someone asks me how I am able to get it clean after it receives such deposits of sand. In reply, I lift the ramrod which I am holding (or point to it where it stands in the corner) and say, 'I clean it with the ramrod', meaning (and further explaining if I am required to do so) that I hang the rug across the clothes-line and beat it with the ramrod. It seems most unlikely that Shawnee *nipēkwālakha* would be a suitable translation in such a case.

It is worth mentioning in passing that on the (admittedly skimpy) evidence provided, it seems most implausible that one could find a Shawnee expression which would have the same 'truth conditions' as the English sentence (i.e. would be true in all and only the actual conditions under which the English sentence would be true), or that any English expression could approximate the truth conditions of the Shawnee. It is the contention here that this situation is the normal one — it is what is to be expected unless special factors intervene.

But we have so far defined paraphrastic translation only as translation in which the translation equivalents are not isomorphic. On what basis, then, can they be said to be equivalent? What is implied by an assertion that paraphrastic translation is always possible? Is the claim that for any linguistic expression in any language it is possible to find in any other language a linguistic expression with the same content even when no isomorphic conceptual event is possible? But what could such a claim mean? How is the identity of content to be determined — by some kind of logical calculations? If so, what is the specific nature of the calculations involved, and who is qualified to perform them? And in the end could they appeal to any language-independent conception of meaning, other than truth conditions, which (I hope) was disposed of in the last chapter? There simply do not appear to be any answers to these questions.

As we have seen, the problem is not that linguistic expressions such as sentences do not have meanings. The problem is that these meanings, except in special circumstances — the circumstances which permit isomorphic or near-isomorphic translation — cannot be made commensurable.

Before leaving the subject, we should mention in passing what is sometimes presented as a somewhat weaker claim — the claim (and here we may recall Whorf's sentence about cleaning the gun with the ramrod) that for any linguistic expression in any language which is actually used in a particular context and situation, it will be possible to find in any other language a linguistic expression which will convey the same meaning *when used in an equivalent context and situation*. But this weakened version of the claim still seems to require meaning to be equated with truth conditions, and, in addition, it seems to require an assumption that there are cross-cultural equivalences in contexts and situations. It would be interesting to see an attempt made to define such equivalences. In sum, this weaker version offers no solution to the problems of incommensurability and, in the final analysis, it appears likewise to make no coherent claim at all.

There is, however, a quite different interpretation of the claim that paraphrastic translation is always possible, which perhaps lends itself to confusion with the version which we have just discussed. In this interpretation the claim is not really about linguistic expressions or translation equivalents, or indeed, about meaning at all. It might be stated in something like the following form: no matter what one might need to communicate in any language, it is always possible to find a way to get it across. Differently put, the claim seems to be that it is possible to make anything understandable to any audience in a language which the audience understands. Since the claim concerns what it is possible to accomplish by means of language, we might call it the claim of *perlocutionary intertranslatability*. Now, it is worth mentioning again that this version does not necessarily contain any claim about linguistic form. It is not even necessarily restricted to cases where the source and target languages are different (or even to cases where there *is* a source language).

Since it makes no claim about meaning or about language as such (as opposed to language use), the perlocutionary-intertranslatability claim appears to have nothing to do with the choice between the mapping and reality-construction views of language. However, it is an interesting claim in its own right. In order for it to be evaluated, it seems necessary to make clearer what is intended by the assertion that one can make an audience understand what one tells them, i.e. to make clear what criteria an audience has to meet in order to be said to have understood. But this is not a simple question.

Understanding

The question of understanding something which has been said has come up in two connections. First, it was pointed out that all paraphrastic translation requires that the translator understand the original, and secondly, we saw that there is the perlocutionary-intertranslatability claim which specifies that an audience can be made to understand the translation. Therefore, it seems important to pause a moment to consider what it means to understand something which has been said. One point which may very appropriately be made to begin with is that the mapping view of language virtually ignores the part contributed by the hearer to the process of verbal communication. It is true that, with its disposition to focus on the linguistic expression (conceived of as autonomous text) and real-world situations and to view them as constituting a two-place relation, the mapping view tends to downplay the part of the sayer as well. However, his/her role in designing the linguistic expression is at least tacitly acknowledged, while that of the hearer/understander tends to be overlooked entirely.

What at least seems to be the reason for this neglect is easy to discover. It is the notion of autonomous text. In autonomous text, the text proclaims its own meaning. There is no need for an intelligence on the receiving end, no inference for that intelligence to perform. The meaning stands there, proclaiming itself.

Real language use is quite different. One begins with purposes which one seeks to satisfy. One develops strategies for satisfying them or for improving one's position for satisfying them in the future. A single strategy is likely to envisage several purposes at the same time. Some strategies include saying something as one of their components. In these cases, one designs a linguistic expression to contribute its allotted part to the overall strategy.

This expression comprises a conceptual event, hints as to what it should be interpreted as relating to (what we have called its 'contextualization'), and a modality. But in addition to these things which I have collectively referred to as its 'content', it will probably contain indications of the speaker's attitude toward the addressee, other persons present, persons under discussion, the situation in which the speech event takes place, etc., or even all of these. These indications taken together might be called its 'sociolinguistic meaning'.

In addition to all of these aspects of the design of the expression, it will also incorporate what we may call an *expository strategy*. The expository strategy is a deliberate shaping which is designed to influence the process of understanding by the hearer. I do not know very much about this subject, but it is very definitely an important one and one that is likely to be largely ignored until we adopt a view of language which acknowledges the part played by the hearer.[9] Perhaps the most obvious aspects of expository strategy are the deliberate highlighting of one assertion and the downplaying of another, or the choice of one proposition to be openly asserted and another to be slipped in as a presupposition.

To understand something, it has been said, is to 'give it a "reading" in terms of which it "fits" into a larger, coherent, unitary picture of the world'. Moreover '. . . it is the lack of a coherent context which, in general, will be what stands extrinsically in the way of understanding something, which makes it difficult to understand.'[10]

It seems clear that the content of a sentence must be thought of as an abstract representation, and that in order for an act of communication to be completed, the audience must provide this abstract representation with an interpretation. To provide the interpretation is to perform what may appropriately be called the 'act of understanding'. Understanding in this sense is in essence an act of perception — perceiving the significance of what was said. Like all perception, of course, it is fallible.

To discuss perception — and therefore understanding in this sense — requires that we turn our attention temporarily to the part played by the hearer rather than that played by the sayer. Perception is best regarded as a matter of information pickup, that is, of the organism (in this case the hearer) gleaning information from the environment. It is important to keep in mind that whatever a perceiver may choose to focus upon is situated within a broader context. That is, whatever the extent in time or space of the unit which the perceiver determines to focus upon, it exists, and is perceived to exist, within a context in time and space. And this context is part of what is perceived.[11]

A speech act is an unusual challenge to perception in that it involves two kinds of contexts. The first is the *context of the speech act* itself. There is, necessarily, some perception of the performance itself — of what the speaker is doing in performing that act. Now one might want to contend that a speech act has not been completely understood until the speaker's motives have been recognized — until we have figured out what he/she is up to. However, that is clearly not the kind of understanding that is involved in translation — surely no one would expect a translation to reveal the hidden motives of the speaker — and presumably the perlocutionary version of intertranslatability would not require that kind of understanding either. On the other hand, we would expect the translation to attempt to reveal those intentions of the speaker which he/she intended to have recognized by the audience. Those intended-to-be-recognized intentions do not seem to belong exclusively to either the first or the second context.

The second context is that of the conceptual event specified in the actual linguistic expression, i.e. the *context of that which is being talked about*. As would be expected from the above discussion of perception, understanding of a linguistic expression which specifies such a conceptual event might require a context involving more inclusive events or situations in which it is nested or events or situations likely to have preceded it or to be consequent upon it. It is this context to which the linguistic expression itself provides clues (i.e. in what we are calling the 'contextualization' component of its content).

The information pickup required for understanding varies widely as circumstances differ. Presumably it always requires some putting into context. Saying something in the first place involves what might be thought of as an impressive feat of abstraction. Understanding what was said involves reversing the abstraction — restoring the context — in some degree. The context which must be restored or supplied may be quite narrow, or it may be very broad.

What determines when enough context has been supplied and understanding has been successfully accomplished? It would seem that from the hearer's point of view it may be considered to have been accomplished when the hearer is satisfied that he/she has understood sufficiently well and turns his/her attention to the next order of business. From the beginning it is the speaker's task to anticipate the strategy which the hearer will employ in seeking to understand and to tailor the utterance so as to exploit that strategy. If the speaker has anticipated inadequately, what satisfies the hearer as understanding will probably not satisfy the speaker that his/her meaning has been understood. In any case, the translator's role is to bring about the understanding which the original speaker intended, and the translation should be designed according to considerations analogous to those which governed the design of the original utterance. Likewise, one must assume the perlocutionary-intertranslatability claim to envisage criteria for judging the understanding elicited by a translation which would also reflect the considerations which motivated the original speaker.

What does the Intertranslatability Postulate Postulate?

The isomorphic version of intertranslatability is a very strong claim indeed, one which has probably never been explicitly asserted by anyone. And yet, as we saw above, it is the only version susceptible to a sufficiently specific formulation to make possible any clear idea of what might count as evidence for or against it. The perlocutionary version — the claim that it is possible to make anything understandable to any audience in a language which that audience understands — is an interesting claim, but it is not at all clear how it might be tested (or what reason there might be to expect it to be confirmed by an objective test). In any case, it does not seem to contain all of the assumptions that the intertranslatability postulate requires.

Our only basis for determining what assumptions the postulate actually requires is to consider what assumptions are required by the practices which are justified by the postulate. It is apparent in many cases that the translator/interpreter is conceived of as functioning as a *surrogate sayer*. That is, it is assumed that when the translator or interpreter speaks, it is *as if* the audience were somehow empowered to hear and understand the original source-language utterance. It is not uncommon, for example, to hear someone produce an exact quotation from a translation of some work, and refer to that quoted translation as what the author-Jesus, Confucius, Plato, Marx, or whoever-'said'.

The same assumption appears when legal documents are produced in several different languages with the understanding that the text in each language is equally valid. An example of this is the Charter of the United Nations with equally valid versions in English, French, Spanish, Russian, and Chinese. It is assumed that all versions say the same thing.

Another example is provided by the use of interpreters, as, for example, in American courtrooms. A lawyer may ask a question in English of a witness who does not speak English. An interpreter is then supposed to put the question into the witness's language — to say the same thing that the lawyer said, as if the lawyer were saying it, i.e. avoiding any explanation. Thus, the role of the interpreter is that of an other-language surrogate of the lawyer, not that of an intermediary.

The witness then answers, and the interpreter puts the answer into English, again supposedly saying *the same thing* that the witness said except that it is said in English. The court transcript subsequently shows only the lawyer's question in English and the witness's reply in English. The presumption of the legal system is that the question which the witness heard and attempted to answer is the *same* question as the English-language question which appears in the court transcript and that the English reply shown in the transcript *says the same thing* as the witness's original reply.

Procedures such as these seem to offer clear proof of the existence of an assumption that expressions in different languages can say the same thing in the sense of having identical content, and, in fact, that an expression with identical content can *always* be found. Thus, it seems evident that the mapping view of language — the view which characterizes contemporary linguistics as well as our society at large — includes a form of the intertranslatability postulate in which equivalence of meaning between the *actual linguistic expressions* is postulated. And the only condition under which such equivalence of meaning exists is where isomorphism is possible. At least no other tenable basis for judging the meanings of translation equivalents to be even commensurable has been proposed.

Therefore, there seems to be no doubt that the mapping view of language actually requires the postulate of isomorphic intertranslatability. However, the slippery point is that, if the postulate is challenged, its defenders have the option of assuming that it is some other version which they are called upon to defend. The other versions which claim equivalence of meaning between linguistic expressions are very difficult (in fact, presumably impossible) to state in testable form, and because of their very vagueness, they seem very difficult to disprove. But even the perlocutionary version is not easy to state in testable form (the formulation given here — that *anything* can be made understandable to *any* audience — may be stronger than some would accept, but it is not clear what kind of weakening should be considered). The ambiguity provided by these interpretations is what gives the postulate the invulnerability to empirical evidence that is necessary in a postulate.

Conclusions

I believe that what has emerged from the discussion in this chapter and those preceding it is that the intertranslatability postulate is false. There seems to be no coherent interpretation of it and no interpretation which justifies the assumptions required by our institutions by which it could conceivably be true. Unless some weakened version of what was called here the perlocutionary-inter-translatability claim is found to be valid, there seems to be no basis upon which it might be possible to maintain that anything can be said in any language. In any case, there seems to be no foreseeable possibility of defining a version of intertranslatability which would be capable of justifying the institutions which we have built upon it.

But, one may well ask, if languages are not inherently inter-translatable, how is it that institutions and practices such as those described above — institutions and practices which are based on translation — can survive and maintain their credibility? How is it that belief in universal intertranslatability can persist among us?

I believe that the answer given to that question several years ago by Willard Van Orman Quine is the correct one. Quine wrote:

> Translation between kindred languages, e.g., Frisian and English, is aided by resemblance of cognate word forms. Translation between unrelated languages, e.g., Hungarian and English, may be aided by traditional equations that have evolved in step with a shared culture. What is relevant rather to our purposes is *radical* translation, i.e., translation of the language of a hitherto untouched people.

Later he goes on to say:

> . . . containment in a continuum of cultural evolution facili-tated translation of Hungarian into English. In facilitating translation these continuities encourage an illusion of subject matter: an illusion that our so readily intertranslatable sentences are diverse verbal embodiments of some intercul-tural proposition or meaning, when they are better seen as the merest variants of one and the same intracultural verbalism.[12]

I think that we may go on to observe that Quine's radical trans-lation is practically unobtainable in the world of today. As Quine noted, the constructed realities represented in English are to a large extent shared with other European languages, even unrelated ones such as Hungarian. In short, we can quite appro-priately speak of a constructed reality shared with minor variations by the speakers of all of the European languages — a constructed reality of Western culture. But today, this 'Western' culture has expanded to embrace almost the entire world — it might more appropriately now be thought of as simply the culture of the modern world. The modern world is a world of shared subject matters and shared ways of talking about them, i.e. ways of talking about them which are diffused in large part by calquing from one language to another. To give intertranslatability anything approaching a fair test would require that one of the languages represent a culture which has remained unaffected by the culture of the modern world.

The conclusion that the intertranslatability postulate is false seems clearly to have significant consequences. It means, I believe, that we must rethink the role of language in our lives. We must recognize that each language has a unique potential for reality construction — each subtends a different set of potential realities. Therefore, the loss of any of these is a diminution in the vision of the species.

We must rethink our conception of our relation to the world outside of us and of what we know and can know of it. For it is evident that our *effective* environment is as much our invention as our discovery.

We must rethink our assumptions and practices concerning translation between languages and the assumptions which govern interactions between speakers of different languages (or of significantly different linguistic repertoires) in our society, for there is much injustice there.

Finally, we must rethink our assumptions about the relation between language and thought and the relation between language and culture. For surely language is less separate an entity than our scientific division of labor has assumed.

Notes

1. However, it should be pointed out that even isomorphism between translation equivalents does not assure that the two will be understood in the same way; cf. Grace 1981: 49.

2. Vinay and Darbelnet 1958.

3. Some of my appreciation of the complex demands which understanding makes on the hearer comes from work in artificial intelligence. For example, Roger C. Schank in discussing what artificial intelligence research indicates a computor (or a child) must know how to do in order to understand a simple story, provides the following list (Schank 1982: 15):

1) make simple inferences
2) establish causal connections

3) recognize stereotyped situations (scripts)
4) predict and generate plans
5) track people's goals
6) recognize thematic relationships between individuals and society
7) employ beliefs about the world in understanding
8) access and utilize raw facts.

4. Compulsory categories received particular attention from Franz Boas and his students. Cf., for example, Boas 1911.

5. The reference to *modulation figée* comes from Vinay and Darbelnet 1958. In that work, *modulation* (which is of two kinds: *figée* and *libre*) is defined (1958: 11) as *'variation obtenue en changeant de point de vue, d'éclairage et très souvent de catégorie de pensée'*. The examples of fire-boat, etc. are found on p. 88, and elsewhere.

6. The example of *transposition* ('He limped across the street') was taken from Vinay and Darbelnet 1958: 6.

7. It should be pointed out that some claims for intertranslatability are based on abstracting some kind of essence of the language from its vocabulary. That is, they allow for unlimited creation of new vocabulary through borrowing or whatever in order to accomplish the assigned translation task. However, it seems to go without saying that if enough importing of material into a language is allowed, the language will be able to provide exact translation equivalents of anything whatsoever. This view of what a language (or its essence) is seems to me to be quite mystical. In any case, this kind of claim has no bearing on the institutions and practices in our culture which appeal to intertranslatability for their justification.

Apart from these very abstract kinds of claims, the issues concerning intertranslatability might be described as 'bracketed' in the literature in the works of Willard Van Orman Quine and Jerrold J. Katz. Quine's position of translatability is that 'radical' translation, i.e. 'translation of the language of a hitherto untouched people', is not possible, or more exactly, that what is a good translation and what is not is indeterminate (Quine 1960: 78). These conclusions are well-known and seem compatible with those presented here. A sharply contrasting view which has received a great deal of attention is Katz's 'effability' principle; cf. for example, Katz 1972, 1976, 1978, 1981. This principle has been variously stated; for example in Katz 1976: 37, we find the following: 'Every proposition is the sense of some sentence in each natural language.'

This is clearly a strong version of intertranslatability. Although it does not exclude paraphrase, it does appear to claim a context-independent equivalence of meaning between linguistic expressions. However, as was noted in the text about such claims, it is not at all clear what would constitute evidence for or against the claim, even concerning a single instance, let alone as a universal claim.

8. Whorf's Shawnee example is found in Carrol 1956: 208.

9. Although, as I said, not enough is known about what I call 'expository strategy', I am impressed with the work of a group who worked at the University of East Anglia a few years ago. Cf. Fowler *et al.* 1979 and Kress and Hodge 1979.

10. The definition of 'understanding' is taken from Rosenberg 1981:

33. My discussion of the process of perception was influenced by Gibson 1979. Also influential were George Lakoff and Mark Johnson, who suggest that 'understanding takes place in terms of entire domains of experience' (Lakoff and Johnson 1980: 117). These domains of experience are known to us as what they call *experiential gestalts*. That is, reference to them calls up a whole schema of things which, in our experience, tend to *go together*.

11. There is a great deal of literature dealing with the complex contexts which are invoked in perception, memory, and other psychological processes, although the discussions do not usually focus on the use of language. There is, for example, an extensive literature on concepts such as 'schemata' (a concept due to Henry Head 1920: 605, and Frederic Bartlett 1932: 201 and *passim*) and 'cognitive maps' (due to Edward Tolman 1948). For a more recent account of both of these and other related concepts, see Downs and Stea 1973. I also rather like Julian Jaynes's (1976) term 'narratization' for a kind of interpretive process by which we contrive contexts for experiences of all kinds — contexts which provide rationalizations for them and perhaps suggest what is to be expected next.

12. The Quine quotations are taken from Quine 1960: 28, 76.

Part III

Conceptual Worlds

6

Conceptual Elements

This chapter and the two which follow will be devoted to an account of the conceptual worlds provided by the linguistic resources at our disposal. These conceptual worlds constitute the environments in which, effectively, we live and conduct our affairs. We might, therefore, characterize Part III as concerned with language systems — conceived of as synchronic systems of linguistic resources — and Part II as concerned with language use. However, Part II dealt only with those aspects of the use of language which are involved in its representational function — the entire subject of language use is, of course, very much broader. And Part III omits most of the aspects of structure which are most conspicuous in the synchronic systems which we call languages. The kinds of resources which will concern us here are more characteristic of other kinds of synchronic units, such as the linguistic repertoire of an individual or a community.

The present chapter will be concerned with the most fully conventionalized aspect of the conceptual world, the conventional signs of our language (or of our linguistic repertoire). We saw in the preceding chapters that when we say something, that 'something' consists in large part of what we called a 'conceptual event'. This conceptual event is constructed out of 'conceptual elements' provided by the language and arranged into a structured unit in accordance with the grammatical machinery of the language. Now the conceptual elements out of which the conceptual event is constructed belong to an inventory of conventional elements made available by the language (or the linguistic repertoire). From the standpoint of the language, the conceptual elements appear as the conventional meanings (which I will call the 'senses') of the conventional linguistic signs of the language (or repertoire).

As we saw earlier, linguistic signs may be classified into several different kinds. These differences of kind result from three basic distinctions: 1. sentence-level vs. word-level signs, 2. *ad hoc* vs. conventional signs and 3. motivated vs. unmotivated signs. We will be concerned here with word-level conventional signs, both unmotivated and motivated.

Linguistic signs are usually represented as units consisting of two component parts or poles, a signans (or 'form' or 'expression') and a signatum (or 'meaning' or 'content'). In the preceding chapters we have been concerned with *ad hoc* sentence-level signs, and especially with the conceptual events which are the principal components of their signata. These conceptual events are structures of which the elements are word-level signs. The *ultimate* components of any linguistic expression are, in fact, unmotivated, conventional, word-level signs. The *immediate* components are also word-level signs, but they are not necessarily unmotivated or even conventional signs.

We must distinguish two kinds of meanings in the signata of linguistic signs: the *senses* of conventional signs and the *characterizations* of motivated signs. What seems to be thought of as the most typical kind of linguistic sign is the unmotivated word-level sign. Such a sign has only a sense; it involves no characterization. In such a sign the association of the signatum with the signans is arbitrary (such signs are, therefore, necessarily conventional rather than *ad hoc*). However, many (in fact, surely most) conventional signs are motivated (or more accurately, partially motivated). That is, they are themselves composed of other signs, and these component signs were not chosen at random, but rather were chosen for the characterization which they gave to the element which constitutes (the sense of) the newly created sign. Therefore, their signata comprise a sense plus a characterization. We will return to a consideration of characterization later, but now we will be concerned with conventional senses and the conceptual elements which they represent.[1]

The mapping view of language operates with a conception of word meaning (I will, when no harm seems likely to be done, use the expression 'word' for short in referring to conventional linguistic signs) which might be called the 'constrained-reference' conception. In this conception, it is supposed that for each word there is a certain class of real-world objects (or acts, states, etc.) such that that word may properly refer to any member of that class but to nothing else. Thus, the word has a referential scope which is precisely constrained — confined to the membership of the assigned class of real-world objects, whence the designation 'constrained-reference' conception of meaning.

On the basis of that assumption, it conceives of the meaning of the word (what I am calling its 'sense') as consisting of the principles, the criterial attributes, which distinguish instances in which it is authorized to refer from all other instances. In actual fact, such a view becomes quickly absurd once one ceases to assume that the world is a closed system whose characteristics are essentially known to us already (see the discussion of the implications of the mapping view in Chapter 1).

However, many linguists have appeared to assume that an adequate linguistic description would include a dictionary in which the meanings of the lexical items would be specified to these standards. Given the world as it is, it is not at all clear what this would mean in practice. Would our criteria have to be sufficient to distinguish for each word instances in which reference is authorized from non-instances in all possible worlds or only in some more narrowly defined world? That is, are we to be content with principles sufficient for all immediately practical purposes, or do we want to require them to be sufficient absolutely (in the presence of freaks, very exotic situations, etc.)?

There was a time, or so I read somewhere, when it was widely believed that all swans were white. Whiteness, then, would have been a quite valid criterial attribute for swans. However, in the exploration of Australia black swans were discovered. In effect, the exploration of Australia had created a more inclusive world in which the old criterial attributes for swans no longer were valid. Although we can be quite confident that there are no more continents on this planet which are waiting to be explored, we can also be sure that there are still many discoveries to be made, and that some of them will change our ideas about the universe.

To provide absolutely sufficient principles would be, even theoretically, a virtual impossibility. Principles sufficient for practical purposes are principles sufficient for the cases that actually arise. However, just what these will be can only be determined with certainty *post hoc*. In the present state of our knowledge of the world, this approach to the matter has clearly become unreasonable.

There can be no account from the reality-construction view of the nature of linguistic senses (and therefore, of conceptual elements) that will be comparable in simplicity to that of the mapping view. However, I will attempt to provide some indications of their nature in what follows.

It seems reasonable to take as our starting point the principle that the meaning of a linguistic sign such as a word is whatever one has to know in order to satisfy speakers of the language that one knows the meaning of that word. Moreover, it seems important not to make the tests of that knowledge too stringent, because we do not want to be put in the position of saying that none of, or even that only a fraction of, the people who use a particular word actually know its meaning.

Let us begin by considering some ways in which the mapping view of word meaning (i.e. the view that to know the meaning of a word is to know criteria sufficient to identity instances to which the word may properly refer) is mistaken. Then we will consider a speculative account of the evolution of human language, or more accurately of 'prelanguage', to indicate what kind of thing conceptual elements, and eventually the senses of words, are.

What Word Meanings are not

There are three points to be made about what word meanings are not:

1) Some words correspond to classes of objects (or the like) whose membership is determinate, or at least determinate for all immediately practical purposes (such classes are what I have elsewhere called 'bounded categories'),[2] and some do not. However, it is not necessarily true even where a bounded category is involved and where a particular speaker shows the ability to apply the word to all and only members of the category, that the knowledge which permits him/her to do so is anything like knowledge of criterial attributes.

In fact, I will contend (i) that the ability to identify members of a category is ordinarily simply a matter of recognizing something for what it is — of perceiving *that* a such-and-such is present; i.e. that there is ordinarily no separation in one's experience between sensory data, on the one hand, and inference (applying criterial attributes), on the other;[3] (ii) that such perceptions are indistinguishable from the act of recognizing an individual whom one knows; i.e. that the identification of an object as the member of a category does not involve some principle of 'abstraction' which is different in kind from any principles used in identifying an individual;[4] and (iii) that contextual factors (what was to be expected at the particular time and place) are likely in fact to play as significant a role in the act of recognition as any criterial attributes.

2) However, in the case of some words (i.e. conventional linguistic signs), even though they do designate categories of physical objects, these categories are not bounded ones. Or some may be bounded for specialists (that is, the domain has been formally terminologized by a science or some comparable institution), but not for the ordinary speakers who use the word. An example is my own knowledge of the word 'pine (tree)' in English.

The question is whether or not I know the meaning of the word. It is certainly a fact that I have identified pine trees on many occasions, and that my identifications have appeared to be acceptable to others. However, I am aware that there are many species of conifers which I have never encountered; I know that I am not able to recognize firs or spruces (which do not grow in any part of the world which I know at all well), and I have no confidence that I would be able to distinguish between either of them and pines.

I know that pines, in my experience, have had needles, cones, resin, and a characteristic kind of bark. However, I am not sure whether or not all pines or only pines have these characteristics, or if, in fact, I would be able to tell in all possible circumstances even whether or not these characteristics were present. In sum, if we made the ability to identify all and only the individuals which the word might properly refer to the test for knowing the meaning of the word, then I would not qualify as knowing the word 'pine'.

And yet, if I, who grew up in pine country where I was surrounded by pines and must have had thousands of occasions for referring to them, cannot claim to know the word, how many English speakers could? And 'pine' is certainly one of the few hundred words which would be most widely recognized by English speakers. The conclusion to which we are forced, I think, is the following: if the language — that which linguists described — corresponds to the knowledge of competent speakers, and if people like me are to be accepted as competent speakers with respect to words like 'pine', then criterial attributes are not part of the knowledge which is involved in knowing the meaning of a word.

3) In some cases it would seem very far-fetched to equate the meaning of the word with the considerations upon which one determines whether it is appropriate or inappropriate to use. Surely, if we heard two English speakers arguing as to whether a particular act, the facts concerning which they both knew well, was a 'brave' act or a 'foolhardy' act, we would not take this to be an argument about the facts of the English language or find ourselves obliged to assume that one of them must have a defective knowledge of the language. Determining the proper circumstances for using a word is simply not a matter of being able to identify instances.

Again, we surely would not say that one does not know the meaning of the name of some disease entity simply because one cannot identify instances with certainty. That would be diagnosis, and diagnosis is one of the most difficult skills of modern medicine. *Meaning* is obviously something different. What is it? What form does the sense of a linguistic sign in ordinary natural language really have? Let us consider a speculative account of the evolution of 'prelanguage' to suggest the nature of the answer.

How Languages got their Conceptual Elements

I want to propose a sort of story about the early evolutionary stages of what ultimately became language. It is becoming increasingly clear that our current view of the nature of language more accurately represents the nature of *literate* language, and in particular reflects the tradition of literacy manifested in school systems of the Western world during the last few centuries. However, the advantages of literacy and the standardized languages which it has led to, however great these may be, cannot have been the advantages which led to the evolution of language in the first place. Therefore, although my evolutionary account must necessarily be speculative, I believe that it can provide a useful perspective. This account will look at our ancestors, as I imagine them, at two stages preceding the emergence of language.

The first stage to be considered is that in which the first animal which was capable of learning from experience had just appeared on the scene. The crucial prerequisite for such an animal, I propose, is the ability to perceive *equivalences* in different situations.

Equivalence, for our purposes, may be understood as meaning alikeness according to some criteria. Things are equivalent to one another for some particular practical purpose if they are alike in what is relevant for that particular purpose. It seems reasonable to assume further that the equivalences that these animals recognized and responded to were equivalences in terms of their implications for the subsequent behavior of the animal in question, i.e. something to eat, to seek to escape from, to walk on, to find a way to circumvent, to use for shelter, etc.[5]

An animal which could not perceive such equivalences would necessarily experience each situation in which it found itself as entirely new, as unprecedented in all of its aspects. Since every situation would be perceived as having nothing at all in common with any preceding one, such an animal would be incapable of applying its experience in dealing with one situation to any subsequent one.

It is important to point out here that equivalences are assumed to hold not only between physical objects, but also between acts (for example, there is an equivalence between different acts of eating, an equivalence which is recognized by the existence of the English verb 'to eat'), states, and so on.

There is something else which should also be pointed out here. What makes two situations equivalent in a certain way might be either the presence in each of different individuals of the same kind (say, the presence of one tiger in one situation and a comparable but different tiger in the other) or, equivalently, the presence in both of the same individual (say, a particular tiger). In fact, we may suppose that, for a perceiving animal such as is being depicted here, it would be of little concern whether it was encountering one tiger or many, or even whether there existed only one tiger or many, as long as it or they made equivalent contributions to the situations in which it/they was/were encountered.

We may use the term *kind* to designate a set of equivalent things (or for that matter, equivalent states, acts, etc.). Further, we may stipulate that if any two or more situations are equivalent in some respect, the existence of that equivalence between the situations implies (entails the existence of) a kind. Thus, in the example discussed in the last paragraph, 'tiger' would constitute one of the kinds of things which this animal recognized (although it would have had no name for it, of course) as being potentially recurring features of the world, and that would hold true no matter what that animal might believe about the number of tigers in existence.

81

The second stage to be considered is that which immediately preceded the emergence of language. A particularly distinctive characteristic of our ancestral species, as I imagine them at that stage, was a much greater development of the ability to perceive equivalences, and therefore, to perceive in terms of 'kinds'. We can imagine these animals as living in a world which they conceive of as containing a large number of such recurrent elements, i.e. of kinds of individuals, objects, states, processes, acts, etc., which one might expect to encounter again and again. This set of elements amounts to a kind of ontology, a theory of reality. This theory of reality provides a means for processing and integrating the sensory information received by the animal throughout its life. Presumably some such theories of reality can be attributed to (at least) all mammals, but our pre-language ancestors surely had exceptionally elaborate ones.

Such theories of reality are what we often speak of as 'knowledge' of the world. However, that term is misleading since it implies the accuracy of such 'knowledge'. Still, we may for convenience refer to such theories of reality, which really consist of assumptions, as 'knowledge' of reality. The knowledge of reality possessed by animals at this stage remained essentially private knowledge since they had no effective means of communicating it from one to another among themselves.

That, then, is the proposal as to what conceptual elements are. They are the kinds of acts, objects, processes, states, individuals, etc., which the world is seen as being composed of. And with the emergence of language, they assume the role of senses of conventional signs.[6] However, the conceptual world, at least after the advent of language, is much more complicated than that. It is highly structured, and the first level of structure is to be found in motivated signs.

Motivated Word-level Signs

Linguistic signs have two poles, and the sign may enter our acquaintance by either pole. We sometimes first become aware of a signans and only afterward find out what the sense that goes with it is. That sequence of events is a very familiar learning process. Sometimes, as when a small child is learning everyday words, we think of it as the learning of language itself; sometimes, as in the learning of technical vocabulary in a university science class, we think of it as learning subject matter of some other kind.

There is an opposite kind of situation where it is the signans that we lack — where we have in mind some individual person or object which has no name, or whose name we do not know. Or we may have in mind a kind of thing or a kind of act, etc., which is not recognized in a conventionalized sign of the language (that is, there is no word for it). How do we go about referring to such things?

To begin with, let us distinguish two kinds of situation. First, there is the kind of situation where the speaker sets out to solve the problem once and for all by adding a word (or other expression — in our terms, a conventional linguistic sign = a lexical item) to the language. In one case it might be an advertising agent naming a new product or thinking up some hitherto unrecognized kind of admirable quality to claim for an old one. Or in another it might be a scientist introducing a new concept which is intended to aid in discussing the phenomena he/she studies. We will say more later about the making of new vocabulary.

The second kind of situation is that where the speaker treats the problem as a very temporary one, where he/she is only concerned with finding a way to refer to the thing in question on that single occasion. Let us consider the second kind of situation first.

For such situations, languages provide us with ways of putting together *ad hoc signs*. Ad hoc signs are expressions that are not intended to become permanent parts of the vocabulary; they are intended to be used on just the one occasion. For example, someone might refer to an individual with an *ad hoc* sign such as 'the woman I saw you with last night'.

Ad hoc signs can also be used to refer to types of objects, acts, etc. For example, suppose a couple are looking for a house to rent or buy, and they know what kind of house they are looking for. They might put together this *ad hoc* sign to refer to the kind in question: 'a house with three bedrooms and two baths which is not too far from where we work and is in the medium price range'. It is not surprising that language has no conventional sign for just this kind of house.[7] But it does provide the necessary means for putting together the *ad hoc* sign. That is, it provides various conventional signs ('house', 'bedroom', 'work', etc.) and grammatical means for putting them together.

It is easy to see that the way we go about creating such *ad hoc* signs is by indicating what some of the characteristics of the thing (etc.) in question are. We may say that we characterize it, that a *characterization* of it is one part of the sign.

An *ad hoc* sign has an *ad hoc* signatum. To say that the signatum is *ad hoc* rather than *conventional* means that we are not treating it as a regular element of our world, but only as a type of thing (etc.) that is relevant just this once.

We have now recognized three parts in *ad hoc* signs: (1) a signans, (2) a characterization and (3) a signatum. However, in the case of *ad hoc* signs the characterization and the signatum are precisely identical. An *ad hoc* sign may be said to be completely *motivated*, i.e. it does not mean anything more than what its characterization says. It will be easier to understand what is involved when we have considered conventional signs, many of which are incompletely motivated, i.e. the signatum is not identical with the characterization.

Motivated Conventional Signs

Whereas *ad hoc* signs are always completely motivated, conventional signs run the gamut from those which are completely motivated to others which appear to be completely *unmotivated*, i.e. to involve no characterization whatever. In the latter, the relation of the signans to the sense seems to be completely arbitrary. Examples of such unmotivated signs are English 'head' and 'foot' signifying particular kinds of body parts. As far as we can see, the foot might just as well have been called 'head', and the head, 'foot'.

Unmotivated signs are signs which signify without characterizing. They are usually old ones. When we make up signs for new senses, we very rarely make up completely unmotivated ones. To make up an unmotivated signans, all we would really have to do is think of a combination of speech sounds that is not already a word in the language. For English, an example might be 'splaŋ'. If someone needs a new word for something — that is, if he/she has a sense in mind and needs a signans for it, why should he/she not call it something like 'splaŋ' or 'glub' or 'blick'? (Actually, both glub and blick are already to be found in the dictionary, but I would never have known that if I had not looked them up as I was preparing to write this.) It is a little hard to think up short signantia for English that are not signantia for words already in the dictionary (I am assuming that we will only consider signantia that English speakers would generally find pronounceable — not something like 'ŋsrikn').

However, the fact that such words exist already does not seem to pose a serious obstacle to using either of them as a signans for some quite different sense. There are already many cases in English of words that are alike in pronunciation. Some are distinguished by differences in spelling (pair, pare, pear; piece, peace), but others are alike in both spelling and pronunciation (a bear, to bear; tin can, can = able to). The fact that the new words would happen to be like the other 'glub' or 'blick' in spelling and pronunciation would not be likely to cause more trouble than having two words 'bear' or two words 'can'.

Moreover, it is much easier to think up signantia of two syllables or longer that are not used in any existing words. All in all, it seems that if people wanted to invent unmotivated signs with signantia that were short enough to be convenient to use and yet not likely to be confused with anything else, it would not be hard to do.

However, that does not seem to be a very natural procedure. For example, suppose that a new kitchen gadget is put on the market under the name 'blick'. Unless we have already been reached by advertising and told something about the gadget — especially what it is good for — we are likely to look to the signans itself for some clue as to its meaning. People in our society, at least, are likely to assume that such a word is motivated, and to approach it with the idea that its motivation is a puzzle to be solved. If we cannot solve it, we suspect that there must be a key of some kind which we do not have. There must be, we are likely to feel, some word or words in English or some other language which would permit us to see the solution to the puzzle if we could but find them. A most likely hypothesis nowadays is that it is an acronym for something. It seems to me that ordinarily people in our society would be quite surprised to find out that the words had been chosen arbitrarily. In short, we do not expect new signs to be unmotivated; we expect them to provide a characterization of whatever it is that they signify.

Partial and Complete Motivation

We saw above that characterizing something is telling what some of its characteristics are. In producing an *ad hoc* sign, we may give a good bit of detail as in our example of the couple's characterization of the kind of house they were looking for. However, a sign of that length would be inconvenient for a conventional sign, since a

conventional sign is intended to be used again and again. Therefore, conventional signs are usually comparatively short (a frequently used shortening device when conventional signs are too
long is the acronym). Still, they do very often consist of more than
one word. 'White House', 'House of Representatives', 'sacrifice
fly', 'to ground out' are examples of conventional signs consisting
of more than one word each.

At this point it may seem unclear just how it is possible to tell an
ad hoc sign from a conventional sign. The answer is that there is
often no way to tell just from hearing the sign used, and that confusion is of considerable value to those in advertising and other
persuasive professions. The key difference between the two, of
course, is that the conventional sign is an established unit even
though it may be made up of more than one part. Moreover, *ad hoc*
signs always have signantia that are completely motivated while
those of conventional signs often are not.

We can distinguish three kinds of conventional signs according
to the degree of motivation. As we saw above, some conventional
signs are completely unmotivated. Examples given above were
'head' and 'foot' signifying particular parts of the body. In addition, there are conventional signs which are partially motivated
and others which are completely motivated.

The existence of signs which are at the same time both conventionalized and completely motivated is a very important fact for
understanding how language works, but it is often overlooked.
Examples abound in such works as Eric Partridge's *A Dictionary of
Clichés* or *A Dictionary of Catch Phrases*.[8] However, many of the
clichés and catch-phrases cited in these books are incompletely
motivated — in fact, it is difficult to select particular items to serve
as examples of completely motivated signs and feel confident that
they will be acceptable to everyone. Still, I will propose that clichés
such as 'the acid test' (or catch-phrases such as 'Don't spare the
horses') are not completely motivated — that knowing the
meanings of the constituents is not enough to permit one to use
and understand such expressions in the way that a fully competent
speaker of the language does. By contrast, I propose that clichés
such as 'casual remark', 'the discerning reader', 'inevitable consequences', 'irreparable loss' (or catch-phrases such as 'I'm a
stranger here myself') are both clearly conventionalized (i.e. we
recognize them as familiar expressions and some of them doubtless
spring readily to our lips) and also completely motivated (i.e. they
have no special meaning which a speaker needs to learn over and

above the meaning contained in the meanings of their parts).

One additional example has been suggested by Charles O. Frake.[9] In discussing the categories available to someone in an American lunch-counter, he mentions such kinds of sandwiches as hamburgers and ham and cheese sandwiches. It is clear that 'hamburger' is a conventional sign and that it has a sense which could not be predicted from its characterization (if, indeed, it can be said to contain a characterization at all). 'Ham and cheese sandwich' is different.

Its signatum does not appear to be anything which would not have been anticipated from the characterization which it provides. However, there are two reasons why we must consider it to be a conventionalized sign. First, it has become a fairly standard item on sandwich menus. Secondly, its signans has become conventionalized; it would be somewhat unconventional, for example, to call it 'cheese and ham sandwich'. Therefore, even though it does not appear to have a sense that involves anything more than might have been predicted from the characterization, the sign is a conventional one because the signans is conventionalized and the signatum itself has become a conventionally recognized entity — a conceptual object — in our culture.

Another similar, and in some respects more convincing, example is the 'bacon, lettuce and tomato sandwich' (which even has acquired an abbreviated version, 'BLT'). It is quite important to recognize that these completely motivated conventional signs function in the same way as do other conventional signs. Their signata are also among the elements of our world. That is, their signata now qualify as 'senses'.

A conventional sign that is partially motivated also provides a characterization of its sense, but that characterization is incomplete. That is, it provides some suggestions as to the nature of the sense. Partially motivated signs take three different grammatical forms.

The first of these differs from the others in that it makes its characterization with a single element rather than assembling it by putting together several parts. It characterizes, in short, by 'extending metaphorically' a signans to an additional sense. It thereby suggests that the nature of the second sense is somehow comparable to that of the first. Examples of conventional signs of this type are 'head' (of a bed), 'foot' (of a bed), 'foot' (of a mountain), etc. These signantia characterize their senses by representing them as comparable to a (real) head or a (real) foot.

The other types assemble their characterizations out of two or more parts. In the first of these types, the resulting sign is a single morphologically complex word. Examples are 'football', 'pineapple'. There is a very common pattern in the Western world of making up new words out of parts taken from Latin or Greek. Some familiar examples are 'anthropology', 'automobile', 'condominium'.

Conventional signs of the remaining type are made up of more than one word. It is conventional signs of this type that are hard to distinguish from *ad hoc* signs. These signs are what are commonly referred to in linguistics as *idioms*. Since the sense of an idiom cannot be determined (at least, not completely) from the senses of its parts, it is necessary to include the idiom and its definition in the dictionary if we are to give a complete description of the language.

We have already seen a number of examples of idioms in these pages: e.g. White House, House of Representatives, to ground out, sacrifice fly, or infield fly rule, grade point average. All idioms, of course, comprise a characterization as well as a sense. They differ widely in how effectively the characterization suggests the signatum, however. In some cases, if we heard the idiom used in the right kind of context, we might guess its sense quite accurately. For example, if someone was listening to a discussion of the structure of the legislative branch of the United States government, and at some time the idiom 'House of Representatives' was used without explanation, the listener might well infer that it was the designation for one of the two 'houses' of Congress — in fact, for the one *not* called the 'Senate'.

At the other extreme are idioms in which there is no obvious connection between the characterization and the sense. Examples are: Texas leaguer (a ball hit into the air in baseball which falls between the infielders and the outfielders), (to be) from Missouri (skeptical). Presumably in most such cases the characterization was once connected to the sense by some allusion, the key to which is no longer common knowledge. Incidentally, such use of allusion is, itself, a kind of metaphorical extension.

Signs and Senses

A single signans may be paired with more than one sense, and therefore participate in more than one linguistic sign, since each different pairing of a signans with a sense defines a different linguistic sign. Therefore, what is represented in conventional dictionaries as a single lexical item may have a number of different senses (be a number if different linguistic signs) — each different 'meaning' defined for such an item in the dictionary being a different sense.

An analyzable (into words or morphemes) sequence has acquired a (holistic) sense of its own if its signatum is no longer predictable from the senses of its parts. An unanalyzable entity, or an analyzable entity which already had a holistic sense, has acquired a new sense if its meaning has been extended in such a way as to require an additional definition in its dictionary entry (i.e. the new sense is an extended meaning, a metaphorical extension).

Conclusions

Let us review what we have said about the linguistic sign. First of all, a language provides an inventory of conventional signs. This inventory of signs is the vocabulary of the language. These signs, or more precisely their senses, are available to serve as elements for the construction of realities. However, we saw also that we are not limited to the elements of the inventory of conventional signs. We can make additional elements by assembling *ad hoc* signs. An *ad hoc* sign is a characterization of the element in question. Such a characterization is made up out of the conventional elements of the language. It is, itself, a kind of model. There is presumably no limit to the number of *ad hoc* elements that can potentially be contrived in a language.

We saw also that many of the conventional signs are motivated. That is, such a sign is made up of other conventional signs of the language. The choice of these constituent signs is not random. On the contrary, their senses are deliberately being invoked. The senses of the constituent signs tend to characterize the sense of the new sign — to provide suggestions as to its nature, as to how it should be perceived, as to the attitude which we should assume toward it. They provide it with something analogous to a built-in reputation.

The conceptual elements of the language are the *senses* of its conventional signs. Theoretically, their characterizations are supposed to be irrelevant. We are sometimes wont to say when we have chosen some motivated sign to designate a new concept (conceptual element) which we have coined, that the form of the sign is irrelevant. We might, we sometimes say, just as well have called it 'glub' or something equally arbitrary. However, that is quite misleading. The characterizations are comments on the way the world is structured. We will consider how the world is structured by language further in the next chapter.

Notes

1. There is a somewhat more detailed discussion of word meaning in the chapter by that name in Grace 1981.

2. The notion of 'bounded category' is introduced in Grace 1981. It is described as follows (1981: 80–1):

Categorization by boundary is based on significantly greater similarities among members of the category than between members and non-members. More precisely, a bounded category consists of a set of individuals such that: (1) each member of the category is similar to some other member while no non-member is similar to any member (in the same degree), and (2) any two individuals in the bounded category are connected to each other by a chain of members such that each such member is similar to the next member in the chain. Nature provides many examples of bounded categories. Animal and plant species are supposed to be such categories. Presumably also many languages are so defined. A bounded category has a definition; whether or not a particular individual is a member of the category is determinate.

3. To illustrate the point that there is ordinarily no separation in one's experience between sensory data and inferences based upon them, I like to tell my classes about a cartoon I once saw. In the first panel of the cartoon we are looking through the back window of a car, presumably from a following vehicle. We *see* two people in the car — a man driving and a woman in the front passenger seat. In the second panel, our vehicle has drawn abreast of the car, and we are looking into it from the (its) left. We now see that what we had thought was a woman in the passenger seat is a large, long-haired dog sitting upright on the seat. The point of the story is what I take to be the expected reaction of the viewer, or, if you prefer, my own actual reaction. My reaction was to wonder how I had been mistaken, and to *look back at the first panel* to find out. On looking back there, I discovered that all that was actually shown of the 'woman' was a dome-like shape covered with long hair which protruded above the back of the seat. Such was the actual sensory information from which I had constructed the woman.

But the key point of all of this is that I had to look back at the first panel to discover what that sensory information had been. One might argue that

I had forgotten what it was. I am more inclined to say that I never knew — or if I knew, it was knowing of some unusual kind, a kind of knowing which, among other things, is not accessible to introspection. I can find nothing in what happened that supports the contention that I passed through a stage of taking account of sensory information followed by a stage of applying inference to determine what I was seeing. And, of course, I take my reaction to be exactly the one the cartoonist intended.

4. On the point that identifying an individual's category (i.e. recognizing that the individual belongs to a particular category) is not different in principle from identifying the individual as an individual, consider that the category is often easier to recognize than the individual. Examples would be many sets of identical twins, dogs of a certain breed, animals of a species, etc. It is hard to see how a separate step of 'abstraction' could be involved in such cases.

5. The suggestion that the equivalences to which my hypothesized early animal responded were equivalences in terms of their implications for the subsequent behavior of the animal was inspired by James J. Gibson's concept of 'affordance'. He wrote (1979: 127), 'The *affordances* of the environment are what it *offers* the animal, what it *provides* or *furnishes*, either for good or ill . . .', and he noted further (1979: 134), '. . . what we perceive when we look at objects are their affordances, not their qualities.'

6. Notice that the idea that conceptual elements (and hence, later, word senses) are 'kinds' (of things, states, acts, etc.) has much in common with what is called 'prototype' semantics. Cf. especially many works by Eleanor Rosch, e.g., Rosch 1975.

7. As Karl E. Zimmer (1971) has noted, it does make a difference whether the audience takes a sign to be *ad hoc* or conventional. Conventional signs are taken to invoke a relation which is 'appropriately classificatory. Zimmer notes (1971: C15):

The dimension of classificatory relevance that I am trying to define here has something to do with the distinction between naming and description. Anything at all can be described, but only relevant categories are given names (I am talking about common rather than proper names).

8. The works by Partridge are Partridge 1962, and Partridge 1977.
9. The paper by Frake is Frake 1962.

7

Ways of Talking about Things

It is primarily in this chapter that we will consider a problem which is actually a very familiar one, but one which has received very little attention from linguistics. The problem is that, in order to speak and understand a language correctly, we have need of a kind of knowledge other than that contained in grammars and dictionaries. In the right circumstances the necessity for this kind of knowledge becomes readily apparent.

To be more precise, in order to use a language correctly, more than one kind of additional (to grammar and dictionary) knowledge is required. First, there is the now familiar claim that all human beings have innate linguistic knowledge of a general sort (i.e. knowledge of principles of language, not pertaining to any particular language). It is certainly possible to interpret that claim in such a way that it is true, but that is not the kind of knowledge that I have in mind. It is also true that there is much complex social knowledge which is necessary if one is to avoid socially inappropriate verbal behavior — knowledge which is required for 'communicative competence'. But that is not what I have in mind here, either.

A third kind of requisite knowledge that is sometimes discussed is 'knowledge of the world'. This is often contrasted with 'knowledge of the language'. This knowledge of the world comes closer to what I have in mind. However, two qualifications are required: (1) that the 'knowledge' is fallible (i.e. it is really a matter of assumptions about the world rather than of what is known with certainty) and (2) that it is really 'knowledge-how' rather than 'knowledge-that' — that it really amounts to knowing how to talk about the subject matters of which our effective worlds are constituted.

The existence of this kind of knowledge is perhaps best illustrated by the familiar fact that it is rare that a literal, i.e. word-for-word, translation from one language into another is idiomatically acceptable in the second. In some cases, the literal translation violates some grammatical rule. However, often it is grammatically impeccable, but there is something else wrong with it. Quite often, it seems destined to evoke the wrong interpretation ('if you said that, people would think you meant . . .'); in other cases, it is just strange ('but we wouldn't say it that way; we would say . . .'). The problem which this raises is that of what Andrew Pawley and Frances Syder have called 'nativelike selection'.[1] They have illustrated the problem by presenting numerous examples of well-formed sentences in English whose meaning is perfectly clear, but which sound strange and unnatural — sometimes extremely unnatural.

Another illustration of the necessity for linguistic knowledge other than grammatical and lexical knowledge presents itself when one attempts to interpret texts in a strange language. Linguists in the course of describing languages in various parts of the world often publish texts recorded in those languages along with 'interlinear', that is, literal, translations. I find that when the language is one that I have no familiarity with, I usually cannot get any reliable idea of what the speaker intends to convey from the literal translation. It is only when I have seen a free (more idiomatic) translation into English (that is, what we have called a 'paraphrastic translation' which tells me in terms which I can understand what the speaker was getting at) that I can begin to make some sense out of the *way* in which it was said. And yet, all of the necessary grammatical and lexical knowledge was presumably provided in the interlinear translation or otherwise made available at the start. The knowledge which I lack in such cases is of another sort. It falls into the realm of what I have called 'idiomatology'.[2]

(It is appropriate to recall here that not only is a word-for-word translation usually incomprehensible, but that even an isomorphic translation will usually not be possible or acceptable. In other words, as we saw in the chapter on translation, no generalizations can be made about the strictly linguistic relations between the expressions in different languages which are capable of serving as translation equivalents.)

Finally, consider one quite different kind of illustration of the need for knowledge other than that of grammar and vocabulary. It was brought out particularly in Thomas Kuhn's *The structure of scientific revolutions.* In that book he pointed out that one of the notable characteristics of a scientific revolution in progress is the inability of the members of each of the competing schools to understand the statements made by members of the other. And yet it is to be presumed that the members of each school are highly competent in the grammar and vocabulary of the language being used (e.g. English in a large proportion of recent cases). It is not difficult to find examples of such misunderstanding between members of different schools, and the misunderstanding is often of a very fundamental sort.

The conclusion must be, then, that our ways of talking about things are not completely accounted for by our grammars and our lexicons. In this chapter we will consider how they are constituted. Probably the best way to introduce this subject is by continuing our hypothetical account of the evolution of language. Let us consider the relevant characteristics of our previously posited hypothetical ancestors in, respectively, their last prelinguistic stage, their earliest linguistic stage, and, finally, in the subsequent evolution of language.

The Last Prelanguage Stage

We last left our ancestors at a stage just before the emergence of language. They could not speak, but they had rich inventories of conceptual elements. However, these animals undoubtedly did communicate with one another about other things. Judged by any non-human standards, the species surely was capable of rather complex communication. For one thing, they probably employed a series of calls — calls which may have been produced involuntarily. However, the primary means used in this communication must have been display — gesture-like use of physical postures and actions.

As a rough characterization, we might say that an individual of this population indicated an attitude toward another by means of a display behavior which suggested (usually by partially acting it out) some less restrained behavior which might potentially be directed toward the other. An example would be baring the teeth as a signal of a predisposition to attack.

It has been said that such communication (and for that matter all mammalian communication) is essentially about relationships.[4] In fact, these kinds of communication continue in modern human

94

beings, and indeed are much enriched by language, which now adds speech acts to the inventory of actions which may be adumbrated in display.

Earliest Language

The next stage to be considered is that in which something that we would be prepared to call language has already appeared. There are two characteristics which must have been crucial to the existence of full-fledged language. The first is the conventional assignment of signantia to conceptual elements of the (thitherto private) ontologies, thereby yielding conventional linguistic signs. The second consists of principles to permit the combination of two or more conventional linguistic signs into larger structures capable of serving as the vehicles of speech acts.

At least two quite different functions would have been required of these combinatory (syntactic) principles at a quite early stage (without them it is doubtful that what we would be dealing with would be judged to qualify as language). The first such function is the characterization of *ad hoc* elements and events in terms of the ontological elements (the 'kinds') made available in the conventional signs of the language.

The second function is the specification of what we have called a 'modality' — i.e. the specification of the condition of instantiation of the conceptual event — which makes saying something in a human language so different from the indicating or hinting which is apparently all that other mammals are capable of (and which humans can also do, of course). One natural concomitant of the specification of the modality, as we saw, is a kind of assumption of responsibility — an explicit commitment — by the speaker (sayer). (A third syntactic function that must have been discernible at a very early stage would be that of providing clues for what we have called 'contextualization', but there is no need to say more about that here.)

The assignment of signantia to conceptual elements marks the inception of *public* knowledge, i.e. of *shared* ontologies. At this stage (we may suppose) the private ontologies tend to merge into a shared community ontology. To begin with, these private ontologies, or the elements thereof, are put on display whenever one talks, because talking involves interpreting whatever one is talking about in terms of the elements of one's ontology. However, in order to understand what another person says, one must be able to interpret with some degree of accuracy the elements which that person uses. Therefore, the requirements of communication surely led individuals to gain familiarity with one another's elements and gradually to develop a shared inventory — a shared ontology. This shared community inventory of elements itself becomes the first public knowledge. At this point in the sequence cultural evolution begins.

We may speculate that language at this early stage would already have become different in different communities in that signantia (and the specific articulatory skills which were developed in order to produce them fluently) would differ from one community to another and the syntactic devices and the inventories of elements would also differ somewhat. In short, there would have been different languages. It is to be noted that the differences envisaged here are on a very primitive level, but that it is also a highly internalized one. Such differences of course continue to exist today, and, in fact, constitute the main classificatory criterion applied to human language by linguistics and in the popular mind. That is, language is classified (or supposedly classified, because in practice the classification cannot always be performed neatly) into individual languages.

How did such languages work? To begin with, the inventories of elements would presumably have been quite small and most of the elements which were present would have been of the sort which are now generally thought of as belonging to the *basic* (or *core* or '*non-cultural*') vocabulary.[5] By the same token, the syntactic constructions would presumably have been comparatively simple. However, they would have been sufficient to permit their speakers to characterize a real or other imaginable situation or event in terms of the elements provided by the language in relationships characterizable by its syntactic resources.

In a language with such limited resources it would undoubtedly have been easier to talk about some things than others. It might, for example, have been easy to talk about weather conditions, but it surely would have been difficult to talk about plate tectonics or sociobiology or the relative merits of different chess openings. Still, what it was possible to talk about could not have been limited to some closed set of subjects or the system would not have qualified as language in human sense. With some ingenuity it must always have been possible to extend the range of what could be talked about — to talk about new and untried subjects. Further below we will consider how this is done.

The Subsequent Evolution of Language

The last stage to be discussed consists of the entire period subsequent to the first appearance of full-fledged language. What I want to propose here is that the most significant kind of development throughout this period was the invention of new ways of talking. Of particular interest from the point of view taken here were ways of talking about new things — things for which there was previously no way of talking. And of particular interest among these are ways of talking about cultural things, i.e. about things which themselves did not exist until humans invented them.

As we have seen, it is often suggested within the framework of the mapping view of language that the principal semantic differences that exist among human languages are to be attributed to different languages' dividing up the world in different ways. But, as I have tried to show, that is a most misleading suggestion. In fact, most of the semantic differences which are of the greatest significance involve ways of talking which are designed for talking about 'things' which have been created within particular cultures, not about things existing in some universally shared world. To the extent that such subject matters are concerned there is no shared world to divide up.

Moreover, it is true that each individual has his/her own repertoire of ways of talking but that the repertoires of some individuals are, nevertheless, more alike than those of others. However, it is misleading to suggest that these differences in repertoires of ways of talking are simply attributable to different languages. In fact, one of the major implications of this account is that the kinds of differences which give us different languages are differences of a very primitive kind, although (or perhaps we should say, 'and consequently') they are the most completely internalized differences for their speakers.

Although the phonological, and to some extent the syntactic, systems do evolve in their own way over time, the most significant kinds of innovations in languages after the primitive stage have consisted in the invention of new ways of talking. And these new ways of talking are not language-specific in the same way in which, say, pronunciation is. Under favorable circumstances they can be adapted easily from use in one language to use in another. In fact, a major instrumentality in the adaptation to Western culture of the countries of Asia has been the importation of ways of talking about things from Western languages into their own languages. Moreover, the development of a new way of talking about something can take place simultaneously in more than one language (as in the development of a scientific discipline).

Thus, it is very common for what is essentially the same way of talking about something to be available in more than one language. It is likewise very common for one speaker of a language to have a particular way of talking in his/her repertoire while another speaker of the same language does not.

What is a Way of Talking about a Thing?

Let us begin the answer to that question by reviewing some of what we said about linguistic signs in the last chapter. First of all, a way of talking about something involves an inventory of *conceptual elements* (mostly kinds of individuals, objects, acts, processes, states, and the like) which are the *senses* of the *conventional signs* of the language. Many of the conventional signs are *motivated signs*. That is, the relation between the signans and the sense is not completely arbitrary. Motivated signs either involve metaphorically extended meanings of other signs (as 'foot' of a bed) or a construction composed of two or more other signs (as in multimorphemic words or idioms). Motivated conventional signs *characterize* the conceptual elements which they represent.

The *signatum* of a motivated conventional sign therefore consists of both a sense and a *characterization*. The signatum of an unmotivated conventional sign consists only of a sense. Signs which are not conventional signs (e.g. most phrases and sentences) are called *ad hoc signs*. Since an *ad hoc* sign has no conventional sense, its signatum consists *only* of a characterization.

New conventional signs are nearly always motivated. That is, they not only name the new element, but they also suggest *what it is like*. All such characterization is at bottom metaphoric, including that of *ad hoc* signs. Consider first what is sometimes called a *root metaphor*.[6] A root metaphor represents one structured *domain of experience* (usually a more abstract one) as being *like* another (usually a more concrete one).

The term 'domain of experience' comes from the book, *Metaphors we live by*, by George Lakoff and Mark Johnson.[7] An example of a root metaphor which they give there is: 'An argument is a building.' Such a root metaphor gives rise to a whole series of what we may call *particular metaphors*: e.g. we can talk about the 'framework', 'solidity', or 'shakiness' of an argument; we can 'construct' it, 'support' it, or 'buttress' it; it can 'collapse' or 'fall apart', etc. That is, we conceive of arguments as analogous to buildings, and talk about them in the same terms. This root metaphor, therefore, plays an important part in strueturing our way of talking about arguments.

Thus a way of talking is based on metaphor, on speaking of one thing in terms of another. To talk about a new subject requires the discovery (invention?) of a suitable root metaphor. At the moment I can say very little about the considerations that govern the establishment of such metaphors. Of course, the metaphor is ultimately to be found in the analogy between the new thing and some familiar domain of experience, but the speaker will presumably want an analogy which presents the new thing in the right light (to suit his/her purposes). At the same time, if the way of talking is to achieve wider acceptance and become conventionalized in the community, it must also be found apt by others.

What are the 'Things' that we Talk about?

To say that different topics of conversation — different subject matters — require different ways of talking seems to suggest that there is for any given community some fixed number of conventional subject matters. If that were true, that number would at the very most have to be finite or speakers could not be expected to learn the appropriate ways of talking for each. But can it be true that there is such an inventory of subject matters, each with a way of talking consecrated to it? It can be said to be true if we regard the system of subject-matter-consecrated ways of talking as an open system as I suggested earlier in the book. Open systems, as we said there, are 'systems which do not have clear boundaries — where some things belong to the system more clearly than do some others and still others may not belong at all, although there is no (non-arbitrary) basis for saying for sure'. That is, we may consider it to be true if we find that convenient, but we must be willing to reckon with a fair degree of indefiniteness in the identification and characterization of the particular subject matters and particular ways of talking.

Some are more highly conventionalized than others. Those which are most ritualistically conventionalized stand at one extreme; at the other are those which are no more than tendencies toward conventionalization. There is a tendency within groups of people and even within single conversations for conventions to begin to take shape. And from the perspective of the community as a whole, certain subject matters will tend to come up repeatedly in conversation, and the way they are talked about and, in general what is said about them, will tend to assume a kind of patterning. If we chose to do so, we might more or less arbitrarily settle upon some kind of criteria which would permit us to say at a certain stage in this development that a new conventional subject matter had come into existence in that community. If (as I am assuming would ordinarily be the case) it were possible to discern particular patterns in the ways of talking consecrated to such a now-conventional subject matter, then we could say that that subject matter governed its own way of talking — that there was a 'consecrated way of talking' about it. If we were to settle upon such largely arbitrary criteria, it would therefore be possible to say that there was a certain fixed number of conventionalized subject matters and of consecrated ways of talking about them.[8] However, there seems to be no immediate value in undertaking to do so.

There is another problem about the definition of conventional subject matters and of ways of talking. As we saw earlier, it sometimes seems convenient to be able to talk about *different* consecrated ways of talking about the *same* thing — the same subject matter (the classical case, for example, being the aftermath of a Kuhnian scientific revolution) — and also to speak of the *same* way of talking about a particular thing as being common to different languages (as, for example, the way of talking peculiar to a particular religious orthodoxy or scientific tradition). The problem is, what (if anything) does it mean to say that two subject matters or two ways of talking are 'the same'?

First, what can it mean to say that two ways of talking are talking about the same thing? That is, what is it to say that two subject matters are the same? I think the answer to this question must be that no two ways of talking are ever about absolutely the same thing. That must be true because, in the final analysis, the thing which a way of talking is about is a thing created by the act of talking about it. Therefore, if two traditions of talking are independent of each other in the slightest degree, their common creature will commence immediately to evolve in slightly different ways.

However, that conclusion does not seem to dispose of the issue. Two schools of linguistics, for example, would both say that 'language' constituted their subject matter. According to what we have just said, however, what is called 'language' in each case is a conceptual object which has the characteristics attributed to it by the assumptions of that school. Thus, the 'language' which is discussed in terms of the mapping view is significantly different in nature from the 'language' of the reality-construction view. And yet it is not entirely accidental that these two objects happen to go by the same name. Certainly the 'language' of the mapping view comes closer to being the same object as the 'language' of the reality-construction view than it does to being the same object as anything that goes under the name 'apple' (whether fruit or computer).

It would appear, in short, that absolute identity is not the only consideration, but that there are also various degrees of alikeness. Although different schools of linguistics may have distinguishably different ways of talking about their object, and consequently, distinguishably different objects, there is much that is common to all of their ways of talking. That which is common to all may quite fittingly be thought of as constituting another, more generalized, way of talking, with the particular ways of talking of the particular schools being simply subvariants.[9] Thus, we may go on to say that there is an object called 'language' which is the object of linguistics as a whole, and other objects called 'language' which are the objects of the separate schools.

To put it differently, we may say that two expressions or two ways of talking may be treated as being about the same thing whenever, *in the perspective which we are taking at that moment*, the 'things' they are about, i.e. their subject matters, are equivalent.

There is still much that is unclear about the whole subject of consecrated ways of talking about things, but it seems most plausible to think of ways of talking as existing on a scale of generality from the most sharply focused (i.e. those with the most sharply focused subject matters) to the most general. As one proceeds on the scale from general to focused, each succeeding way of talking is a special development within a more general way of talking (or perhaps it can draw upon more than one?).

One can go on, in fact, to speak of an individual language, at least when it has become highly standardized (as English is, or at least the standard varieties of English), as comprising a generalized way of talking itself. To go still further, one can even

101

speak of the languages which belong historically to the same linguistic area (thus presumably the languages of the Balkans or of India, and certainly those of Western Europe) as comprising at a high level of generality a way of talking with its own generalized subject matters.

We are left with one final question: How do we talk about things for which we have no consecrated way of talking at all? It is interesting to note that most of the literature of theoretical linguistics (i.e. literature informed by the mapping view) seems to assume that that is precisely the situation in which speakers-to-be ordinarily find themselves. It is a situation of unusual freedom, but for the same reason, one which demands unusual ingenuity. It is a situation essentially beyond the reach of idiomatology. What, then, is a poor speaker to do in circumstances of such unrelieved freedom?

The answer is that one talks about new things in terms of familiar things. One speaks of them *as if* they were these old things, or at least as if they were characterizable in terms of them. In other words, in such unstructured situations one resorts on a grander scale to the same devices which one employs in any situation which calls for any *ad hoc* sign. That is, one characterizes *ad hoc* elements and, by means of these elements, characterizes a conceptual event.

What one does, in short, is make use of ways of talking designed for, and consecrated to, other subject matters to characterize this unconventional subject matter. And the basis for such characterization is metaphor — one speaks of one thing as if it were another. However, as a new subject comes to be an established part of the inventory of things which customarily get talked about, a way of talking about it tends to become conventionalized.

The basis for a new way of talking, then, is the principle of metaphor, of speaking of one thing in terms of another. When someone undertakes to talk about something new for the first time, that person must apply his/her ingenuity in order to find a metaphoric basis for talking about it. He/she must consider what analogies with old things can be exploited in order to present the new thing in a suitable light (suitable to the purposes of the speaker). However, as a subject matter becomes conventional, as a new way of talking begins to crystallize, the metaphoric base also becomes largely fixed and conventional. In due time, some of the terms used in the new way of talking will be thought of as being used 'literally'.

The Centrality of the Role of Ways of Talking about Things

In the reality-construction view of language, the whole of human language is seen as composed of ways of talking about things. In this view each individual language might be seen as the precipitate from a long accumulation of ways of talking about things, some so ancient that it is no longer clear what things they were originally intended to talk about. To the extent that a language is standardized or at least is homogeneous, it in itself probably represents a very generalized way of talking about things (see above).

The reality-construction view with its key concept of subject-matter-consecrated ways of talking suggests a number of apparent consequences. I will point out some of them.

As has been suggested in some of the earlier discussions, any science can be seen as a way of talking about something. Scientific discourse is a way of talking which has achieved a high level of what has been called 'consensibility',[10] i.e. it embodies agreed-upon criteria for reaching agreement. (However, this characteristic of science is only a difference of degree, not a difference of kind, from other ways of talking about things. Ludwig Wittgenstein has said, 'If a language is to be a means of communication there must be agreement not only in definitions but also [queer as this may sound] in judgments'.)[11] The ultimate case of such agreed-upon criteria for reaching agreement is represented by a mathematical deductive system providing mathematical proofs.

As we saw in the original discussion of the two views of language, ways of talking about things normally reflect assumptions which are often unstated. Thus, they often have deeper implications which may not be fully recognized by those acquiring the particular way of talking. For example, a way of talking about political issues may reflect assumptions about human nature and about natural and perhaps supernatural forces. As a corollary, the way of talking chosen for reporting a specific incident (as in news reporting) may reflect assumptions about the larger context — the political and economic forces at play, for example.

Devising ways of talking about things is one aspect of the process of acquiring understanding of the universe. (It is worth mentioning, however, that developing ways of talking about things is more characteristic of our culture than of most.[12] In fact, our proclivity for analysis which leads us to an ever increasing encroachment upon the domain of the ineffable is one of the characteristics of our culture which is most often cited as objectionable by members of other cultures.)

I have heard it suggested that psychoanalytic theories (e.g. that of Freud) are of value precisely as ways of talking about things — ways of talking taught to the patient by the therapist. Furthermore, we provide formal instruction not only in subjects which are intrinsically intellectual in content, but also in matters of skill such as singing,[13] tennis or archery (where the 'Zen' approach which eschews such talking is seen as a novelty).[14] Our instructional practices are such as to require putting the skills into words; in fact, these verbal analyses are regularly compiled into textbooks which are then used by both teacher and learner in the formal instructional process. In other words, the skills to be learned are analyzed in such a way that they can be talked about *as if* they consisted in the application of factual knowledge.

Still, what we might call 'public understanding' of the universe might be measured as a sum of our ways of talking about things. To contrast understanding with knowledge, we might say that the measure of our public *knowledge* of the universe would consist of a sum of what John Ziman calls 'consensual statements'[15] — that is, statements which are universally agreed to at any given moment (i.e. are universally accepted as expressing demonstrated truths).

On the other hand, the extent of our *understanding* of a particular area of subject matter is equal to a kind of sum of our ways of talking about that thing, that is, to the number of different constructions that we have succeeded in putting on it. Or, to put it differently again, it is equal to a kind of sum of the number of its facets we have been able to bring into perspective.

The supposed virtues of increasing the size of one's vocabulary are really virtues of expanding one's repertoire of ways of talking about things, that is to say, the virtues of a richer conceptual world. A vocabulary test is a crude sampling of one's knowledge of ways of talking about things.

I believe that the reality-construction view and particularly the concept of ways of talking about things throws a new light on some matters which have heretofore seemed puzzling to me.

One matter which has seemed puzzling, to me at least, is the mixed success achieved by attempts to describe the semantic structure of the lexicon of a language. Several schools of thought have had a good deal of success in providing precise specifications of the semantic differences which distinguish the words appertaining to a particular semantic 'domain',[16] and therefore, to specifying the structure of the domain. However, cases have also been found where words of similar enough meaning that it would seem *a priori* that they should surely fall within the same 'domain' do not show any recognizable systematic relations among their meanings. A good example is Ureil Weinreich's set: saturnine, sullen, crabby, glum, sulky, surly, gloomy, morose.[17] The explanation proposed by the reality-construction view would be that only vocabulary items that belong to the same way of talking show systematic structural relations, and that Weinreich's set do not belong to a single way of talking.

A second puzzle would concern the nature of idiomaticity, a phenomenon which we discussed above. That is, why are some sentences which are perfectly well-formed grammatically and lexically — for example sentences produced by literal translation from another language — idiomatically unacceptable? The answer proposed by the reality-construction view would be that idiomaticity is nothing more than conformity to established ways of talking about things. More precisely, to talk about something in a language (say, English) where there is a conventional way of talking about that thing, but to employ an unconventional way of talking about it, is to fail to speak idiomatically (e.g. to fail to achieve idiomatic English).

Another generally puzzling area which we have already discussed at some length in an earlier chapter is translation. I believe that the concept of ways of talking about things does much to clarify what is involved. An important point to note is that a way of talking about something is not necessarily just *in* one particular language. The vocabulary itself — if by vocabulary we mean the signantia along with the signata — is divided up according to different languages. However, translation will predictably be easy whenever the entire discourse to be translated falls within a way of talking that is common to both languages. Ways of talking that are shared by at least two languages are so common as to defy enumeration. Ways of talking about something that far transcend any individual languages are exemplified by sciences, religions such as Christianity or Islam, or political philosophies such as Marxism.

The proposed point of view provides a basis for distinguishing several different kinds of cases: e.g. (1) translation between different languages where the entire discourse to be translated falls within a way of talking that is common to both languages, (2) 'translation' between different ways of talking about the same thing in the same language (e.g. between two competing scientific paradigms), (3) translation into a language which does not have a way of talking about the particular thing (the subject matter), as for example, attempting to translate Einstein's special relativity theory into the Eskimo language (as someone once suggested).

Finally, I believe the concept of ways of talking about things helps to clear up another puzzling phenomenon, that of convergent development between languages, or at least the non-phonological aspects of convergence. In my previous book, I proposed that such convergence consisted of the gradual elimination of the differences between literal and free (i.e. idiomatic) translation between the languages in contact.[18] In the reality-construction view, it will be seen as the development of compatibility among ways of talking, leading ultimately to ways of talking that differ only in their signantia.

Notes

1. The problem of 'nativelike selection' is discussed in Pawley and Syder 1983a.
2. Grace 1981: 43ff. discusses at some length, with a variety of examples, phenomena falling under the heading of 'idiomatology'.
3. On the phenomenon of scientists of different schools 'talking through each other', cf. Kuhn 1970: 109.
4. The point that (pre-human) mammalian communication is about relationships is due to Gregory Bateson. Cf., for example, Bateson 1972: 141, 367.
5. The concept of basic vocabulary was developed particularly in connection with glottochronology and lexicostatistics. A good overview is Hymes 1960.
6. The term 'root metaphor' apparently was originally introduced in Pepper 1957. It has subsequently appeared in various places and has a natural application within the Lakoff and Johnson work (1980) although they do not use it there, I believe.
7. Lakoff and Johnson 1980.
8. It is worth pointing out that if in the future there should appear to be some advantage in thinking of a linguistic repertoire (or even of a language, *per se*) as consisting of a certain fixed number of conventionalized subject matters and of a consecrated way of talking about each, there would be no insurmountable objection to doing so. Although to do so would require us to concede to a certain degree of indeterminacy in our basic units, the concession would be no greater than that which we are already required to make in order to be able to assume that there are a fixed number of languages in the world and that every linguistic expression produced is in one of these languages.
9. Michael Reddy's 'conduit metaphor' (Reddy 1979) seems sufficient

to establish that there is a common generalized way of talking about language, and therefore, that at some level language is the same object for different schools of linguistics.

10. The concept and term 'consensibility' come from Ziman 1978. See also Rorty's (1979) discussions of 'normal discourse'.

11. The Wittgenstein quotation comes from Wittgenstein 1958: 88.

12. On the point that developing ways of talking about things is particularly characteristic of our culture, see Scollon and Scollon 1979: 186 on the Athabaskan pattern of learning skills through silent observation.

13. On verbalization of the skill of singing, cf. Pike 1943: 17ff.

14. For the 'Zen' (non-verbalized) approach to tennis, see Gallwey 1974.

15. For 'consensual statements', cf. Ziman 1978: 6.

16. The notion of semantic 'domains' is found in work sometimes referred to as 'ethnoscience', among other things. See Frake 1961, 1962, Conklin 1962. A somewhat similar approach, mostly by German-speaking linguists, was the theory of semantic fields. A quick introduction may be found in John Lyons' general work on Semantics, cf. Lyons 1977: 250–61.

17. The source of the set of words which have similar meanings, but which show no systematic relations among their meanings is Weinreich 1962: 27. Another such list, this time of verbs (viz. bound, hop, jump, leap, prance, skip, spring, vault), is given in Weinreich 1963: 164.

18. Grace 1981 deals with the phenomena of idiomatology and of convergence between languages in contact in considerably more detail than the discussion here.

8
Conceptual Worlds

It was pointed out earlier that language may be said to provide a medium in which humans construct realities for themselves, and that it is in terms of these constructed realities that they live their lives and conduct their affairs. It was also pointed out that the linguistic construction of reality could be thought of as occurring on two levels. The first is the level of the conceptual event. We saw that in a typical speech act the linguistic expression which serves as the vehicle of that act specifies what we are calling a 'conceptual event'. (Although we decided for convenience to refer to all of them as conceptual events, it was pointed out that some of them might be described more naturally as 'states of affairs' or 'situations' than as 'events' in the strict sense of the word.) This conceptual event, as we saw, is an abstract model of an event-sized bit of reality — not necessarily of actual reality, but of at least conceivable reality.

The second level at which the linguistic construction of reality may be observed is that of the conceptual world. A conceptual world was tentatively described as being the constructed reality reflected by a language as a whole. However, as was pointed out, different individuals or different communities of individuals usually have different linguistic repertoires, and it is just as proper to speak of conceptual worlds which are reflected by particular linguistic repertoires rather than by languages. In fact, the effective world of a particular individual is the resultant of a number of influencing factors, some peculiar to the individual and others shared. The shared factors are shared in widely different patterns. Thus, we might speak of a series of worlds, to a great extent nested one within another, in which we *effectively* live.

The Worlds in which we (Effectively) Live

In a practical sense, of course, reality for a particular individual or group consists of what that individual or group can or does know about actual reality — or better, it is reality 'as that individual or group knows it' (that is, as they assume it to be). There are several levels at which the differences between different realities emerge, and each level defines a 'world' of a sort.

There are, first of all, differences in the sensory data available to different species. It was, a few years ago, a notorious fact that dogs' ears were sensitive to frequencies above the normal human auditory range. Whistles were made to produce sounds which were inaudible to humans but audible to dogs. When such a whistle was blown, therefore, its sound was real for dogs but not for humans. That is, (except for whatever knowledge from non-auditory sources they might have had of it) for all intents and purposes the sound did not exist as far as the human beings present were concerned.

It is intriguing to speculate how reality might be altered for us by other changes in our sensory capabilities. For example, at present our eyes are sensitive to frequencies within a particular range on the electromagnetic spectrum. How might reality be altered for us if they were sensitive instead to X-rays, which would presumably render many more things transparent, or to gamma rays, which would presumably render even the atmosphere largely opaque?

I have taken the term 'world' and the idea that different species, etc. may be thought of as living in different worlds from the work of Jakob von Uexküll. In a book originally published in 1934, he suggested that we might think of different species as effectively living in different *Umwelten*.[1] *Umwelten* has been translated as 'worlds', the English translation of Uexküll's book being entitled, *A stroll through the worlds of animals and men: A picture book of invisible worlds*. Uexküll makes the point which we have just been discussing — that we know the external world through the evidence of our senses and that the sensory apparatus of different species of animals varies greatly. Therefore, for a particular species, the world effectively consists of those kinds of stimuli which its members are able to discriminate in such a way as to be able to react with different responses. He discusses the world of ticks, in particular. Their world is, of course, strikingly different from ours. However, the worlds of some animals are much more like

109

our own — especially those of mammals and, most especially, the apes.

The kind of 'world' which we have been talking about so far is the world which is accessible to our senses. It might therefore be called the *sensible world*. Of course, we could go further and say that not only does each species have its own sensible world, but each individual *member* of a species has a unique sensible world since there are individual differences in sensory acuteness (even among individuals who count as 'normal').

However, in addition to sensible worlds, each individual mammal (to be on the safe side I will not say anything about lower grades in the animal kingdom) has what we may call a 'conceptual world'. As was argued in Chapter 6, any creature which is capable of learning from experience must be able to recognize equivalences between situations and must, therefore, recognize 'kinds' of things, states, acts, etc. These kinds must add up to a set of potentially recurring elements of reality, and that set must add up to an ontology — a theory of reality. This theory of reality is what we will call a 'conceptual world', as contrasted with the sensible worlds which we have been discussing.[2]

Mammals are capable of learning from their individual experiences and thereby modifying their individual worlds over the course of their lifetimes. Therefore, it seems appropriate to think of each individual animal as having its own conceptual world. However, presumably the members of a species would, upon maturity, arrive at similar conceptual worlds. Since the members of a species would share a common ethology and similar habitats, most of them should accumulate very similar inventories of experiences. Thus, it seems permissible to think of the species as well as the individual as having its own conceptual world. However, because of the great diversity in culture and habitats of human societies, the notion of the conceptual world of the species, while valid, is probably less useful for humans than for most species.

The advent of language alters the picture in a fundamental way. The conceptual world of an individual-with-language can include things which the particular individual has never personally experienced. For example, one might imagine children growing up in an environment where some dangerous, but seldom seen, animal (say, a nocturnal predator) exists. Through the intervention of language, children who have never seen the animal might still have it as very much a part of their worlds. But we can go a step further. Our hypothetical predator might just as well have been something which nobody at all had ever seen — even something which did not actually exist — such as a spirit. Whether or not it is a part of actual reality is not relevant to its being part of the conceptual world.

Since these elements in the conceptual worlds of these individuals are taken directly from their languages then, it will be convenient to speak of the conceptual world of a *language* (or by the same token, of a dialect or of the linguistic repertoire of a community) — that is, the conceptual world reflected in, and made available by, that language (or dialect or repertoire). As a first approximation we may say that the conceptual world of a language consists of the set of elements represented by its conventional linguistic signs. But the situation is more complicated than that, as the last two chapters have indicated.

The Worlds of the Individual

The individual human being, then, lives in his/her own unique sensible world, but also in the sensible world of the human species. He/she likewise lives in his/her own conceptual world. It is possible also to talk about the conceptual world of the human species, although as was mentioned above, the diversity of cultures and habitats of different human groups probably makes the concept less useful than in the case of other species. But the human individual is also born into a society which has a linguistic repertoire at its disposal, and he/she is therefore exposed to the conceptual world of the society's language (or linguistic repertoire).

The development of the conceptual world of a human child is influenced by the conceptual world of its language almost from its day of birth. From very early in life it learns to interpret its experiences in terms of the elements of the conceptual world of the language. It even learns to *seek* its experiences — to know where to look and what to look for — in terms of that world. And it supplements its own experiences with vicarious experiences supplied by means of the language and in terms of the language.

Since our experiences are so largely filtered through the conceptual worlds of our languages, it is not surprising that our individual conceptual worlds wind up strongly resembling those of our languages. And the contribution of language to these worlds has permitted them to become extremely different — incomparably more 'abstract' (and sometimes pathologically so) — than those of other species. As Hans Vaihinger has pointed out, just as instruments such as the telescope and microscope have greatly extended the range of our senses, so language by means of its 'thought instruments' has greatly extended the range of our thought.[3]

We observed earlier that we might say as a first approximation that the conceptual world of a language consisted of the set of elements represented by its conventional linguistic signs, but we added that the situation in reality was more complicated than that. We may now consider the additional complications. First of all as we have seen in the last two chapters, many conventional linguistic signs — probably most — are motivated. Motivated signs in some degree describe as well as name the element in question, or, in the terminology which we have been using, they include a 'characterization' as well as a conventional 'sense'. Each motivated sign, by providing a characterization of its object, thereby suggests what it is *like* — how it is structured and/or what it is related to. Thus, since many (if not most) of the conventional linguistic signs of a language are motivated, our repertoire of elements is not simply a list but a highly structured system with complex internal relations among elements.

But even more significant than that is the fact that the things which we talk about are, after all, linguistically created things. And when we create subject matters to talk about, we do this by constructing ways to talk about them.

The conceptual world of a language may be thought of as essentially a repertoire of ways of talking about the subject matters which its speakers have invented (or borrowed from other inventors) to talk about. These ways of talking involve characterization, but in addition to the characterizations found in the motivated conventional signs used, there is also the characterization which occurs in the *ad hoc* signs. That *ad hoc* signs involve characterization has always been obvious, of course. What has not been so obvious is that the characterization in *ad hoc* signs is also governed by conventions to a great extent. However, *these* conventions are too general to be regarded as belonging to the lexicon (at least in any current conception of the lexicon). As we saw in the last chapter, they depend heavily on metaphor, and the term 'root metaphor' has been suggested for the conventionalized general analogy upon which the *ad hoc* particular metaphors which are encountered in everyday language use are based.

It should be evident, then, that the conceptual world of a

language is far from consisting just of a list of the items which make up the universe, but that it contains many and complex indications of how these items are structured, what relations obtain among them, and even what attitudes one should take toward them. However, one should not imagine that such a conceptual world taken as a whole needs to show a high degree of internal self-consistency. On the contrary, individuals do not function in all parts of the world simultaneously, but are concerned with different parts, i.e. with different subject matters, at different times.

There is one final point that should be made. That is that it is human beings who have created the conceptual worlds of their languages, and that human beings can also modify them. It should be made clear that languages (including conceptual worlds) are constantly being modified in use. Language use regularly requires the constructing of *ad hoc* signs. Sentence-level *ad hoc* signs regularly require the construction of conceptual events. Each new conceptual event slightly alters the corpus of examples which are available to illustrate how one talks about that particular subject matter.

Word-level *ad hoc* signs are also regularly invented. Some of these gradually become conventionalized, and also (quite frequently in our society) conventional signs are consciously created by means of the same syntactic machinery. In both instances, these additions to the stock of motivated conventional signs contribute to the system of characterizations found in the language.

In fact, whenever anything slightly novel needs to be expressed, it is likely to be expressed by a slightly novel use of conventional means. But this in itself modifies the system of precedents from which speakers work. If something more radically new needs to be expressed, and if the need is sufficiently persistent, a way will surely eventually be found to express it, and the conceptual world of the language will be modified accordingly. Thus, although the conceptual world as it exists at any particular moment is a strong influence upon our preceptions and our thought, it nevertheless does not confine us in unyielding restraints.

Notes

1. The Uexküll work was originally published in 1934, and appeared in an English translation in 1957 (cf. Uexküll 1957).
2. The 'conceptual world' which I attribute to animals as well as to

humans resembles Jerison's (1973) 'perceptual world'. The difference in terms is partly attributable to the fact that human beings were my original point of departure, and I look at the earlier evolutionary stages from their perspective, while Jerison may probably be thought of as approaching the evolutionary sequence from the other end. However, I also believe that there has been a mystification about supposed differences between perception and conception that we should rid ourselves of.

3. Vaihinger talks about 'thought instruments' (and much else of interest) in Vaihinger 1968.

Part IV

Further Implications

9

The Question of the Relation
Between Language and Thought

Part IV deals with miscellaneous matters. In it we will discuss particular questions which assume a different form in a reality-construction view of language. This chapter is concerned with the relation between language and thought. The word 'thought' in English is, no doubt, a multiply ambiguous one. What we will be concerned with here is the relation between one's language or linguistic repertoire, on the one hand, and the way in which one makes sense of the world, on the other. A main point which needs to be made about this relation is that it is not as mystifying as some of the linguistic literature permits it to seem.

It has seemed in the recent past that whenever this question has come up, the discussion has immediately become embroiled in issues formulated in the aftermath of the early 1950s reprinting of writings of Benjamin Lee Whorf. It has been likely, in other words, to turn to the discussion of a 'Whorfian', or 'Sapir-Whorf', 'hypothesis'. In this context it is often suggested that even if it is true that some kind of causal relation exists between language and thought, any serious investigation of the relation is obstructed by our inability to determine which of the two — language or thought — is cause and which effect. Therefore, further pursuit of the question must be deferred until breakthroughs of some presently unforeseeable kind have occurred.

I have tried earlier in the book to show that this reaction is due at least in large part to the fact that linguistics, and to a great extent our culture as a whole, makes assumptions about the nature of language which are simply incompatible with the facts about language which Whorf was pointing out. Therefore, linguistics and the other similarly affected disciplines were confronted with

117

the dilemma of either finding a way of setting aside the questions raised by Whorf or having their own assumptions gradually exposed and called into question. But, as we have seen, the assumptions which were involved were not assumptions of the problematic kind — that is, hypotheses to be tested; they were of the incorrigible kind — that is, those which are not supposed to be acknowledged and which by the nature of their function necessarily elude exact formulation.

The position taken in this chapter will be that the question of the relation between language and thought is not really a difficult one at all, or, at least, that the general outlines of the answer are not difficult to make out. We will see that there are, in fact, a number of points about the relation of language to thought that are reasonably obvious. These seem to provide an adequate basis for restoring the general question, which is surely a sufficiently important one, to the light of day.

The first point which needs to be made is that the question as to which of the two — language or thought — is cause and which effect is a misleading one. It is surely clear upon reflection both that language affects thought and that thought affects language. We will consider both of these effects in turn.

Language affects Thought

The influence of language on thought is most immediately apparent in any *verbal reports* that we make of our thoughts (or of our experience in general). Any such reports must necessarily be influenced by the language in which they are made.

However, I believe that it is also clear from introspection that experiences which we are going to report verbally are not different in kind from those which we are not going to report. In fact, we do not always know at the time of an experience whether or not we will be reporting it verbally, and furthermore it is clear that often in the case of experiences which, as it turns out in the long run, we never report to anyone, we have been quite prepared to deliver such a verbal report.

In accordance with the reality-construction view, language is assumed to represent a reality which has been created by human beings rather than reflecting some objective external reality. However, even without that assumption, it would still be clear that we could not make sense of, interpret, experience, perceive the world around us in anything like the way we actually do without language. Let us consider a few points in amplification of that statement.

1) To perceive anything at all is to interpret it in such a way as to make sense of it, i.e. we do not just see shifting patterns of light, we see people and objects and actions, etc. At least if we are going to *report* what we see, it is much easier to make use of the concepts which exist in the language, i.e. to describe it in terms of the kinds of objects, acts, etc., recognized by the language.

Let us consider one hypothetical example in some detail. Imagine that we find ourselves describing something which we have witnessed, something which we describe as follows:

'A man was walking his dog in the park when the dog saw a cat and started chasing it.'

In seeking to show to what extent such a statement represents interpretation rather than bare objective reality, one might be tempted to start from the retinal image. I will eschew that temptation. However, even when one leaves out this level of very primitive processing, there is still a lot of interpretation to describe. Consider the following elements in the statement:

(i) 'man'. A familiar kind of object, and we, in our role as speaker have settled for that. We could have elaborated (thereby creating an *ad hoc* kind of object) by saying, 'a small, stooped, gray-haired man', but that would have required extra effort which would suggest that the additional information was of particular importance. It would thereby suggest a different interpretation (different emphasis).

We could also have chosen another conventional kind of object — say, a 'Causasian', or a 'male', or a 'policeman', or (if we happened to know) a 'father'. But each of these choices would have made sense of the situation in a more or less different way.

(ii) 'walking [the dog] in the park'. This is a kind of act that is familiar to us. It seems to have some implications as to motive (for example, if we knew that the dog had run away, and the man had just recovered it and was walking it home through the park, we would not be likely to say that he was 'walking the dog in the park'). Therefore, we are again resorting to interpretation, *beyond what can actually be seen*, on the basis of familiar concepts.

(iii) ' "his" dog'. An interpretation — an assumption that the dog which he is walking is actually his property — based on our idea of how things work, of what is likely. It might be wrong, but it would probably be accepted as a reasonable mistake for which the speaker would be held blameless.

(iv) 'saw'. Even this is an interpretation. First, the dog's behavior leads us to infer that it has become aware of the cat's presence. Secondly, the fact that the choice of sight as the sensory medium involved seems so natural is probably due in part to the particular importance of vision in human sensory perception.

(v) 'chasing'. Again an interpretation. We see the dog run and the cat run in the same direction before the dog. We know that dogs chase cats. The concept is familiar, the term convenient. And this interpretation at once makes sense of both the dog's and the cat's behavior.

These examples seem so obviously straightforward as to suggest that the interpretation is automatic. The point: men, dogs, cats, walking dogs, chasing, etc., are among the kinds of things and acts which are conveniently labeled in our language and which we see the world and its events as being made up of. We naturally resort to such familiar things and acts to interpret whatever sense data we receive at any time. We first try to make sense of what we are seeing in terms of such concepts.

2) This example was a very concrete one, and it might seem that to a considerable extent these particular concepts result naturally from experience (e.g. man, dog, chase, etc.); it is easy to imagine that language is simply conforming to nature there. But again we must recognize that the same cannot be said of many of the kinds of things, states, acts, etc., in terms of which we experience the world. For example, consider, in baseball, 'ground rule double', 'infield fly rule', 'sacrifice fly', or just 'strike'. A person who does not understand these concepts will not have the same perception of what is happening, what people are trying to do, etc. — will not *make sense of* it in the same way at all. An almost unlimited number of examples of other such abstract 'things' could be given; e.g. 'double-digit inflation', 'filibuster', 'phoneme', or 'equi-noun phrase deletion'.

Or consider kinds of speech acts as labeled in English: e.g. bequeath, excommunicate, congratulate, appoint, persuade, authorize; or other (non-speech) acts, e.g. chase, enact (into law), double (a runner) off, shoot someone (to shoot someone would presumably not seem a single act except to a culture which understands guns). These concepts are more suggestive of our shaping nature to our purposes than of shaping our perception to nature. But we also use concepts such as these latter ones in making sense of what we see. In this sense we certainly do live in a world of our own creation — a world which has been created in the medium of language and which is maintained and transmitted by means of language.

3) The influence of language upon thought begins early. Children in the socialization process are influenced by their language. The language they speak (or their speech repertoire) provides an inventory of kinds of things, kinds of states, of acts, etc., that purportedly exist in the world — not with the implication that no others can exist, but probably at least with the implication that these are most of the most prominent ones.

It should be emphasized that language can introduce the child to elements of the world long before the child has encountered them in real life. For example, in the last chapter, the hypothetical case was described of a society which had in its environment a dangerous, but seldom seen, kind of animal (a nocturnal predator, we supposed). Children in that society who had never seen one of those animals had nevertheless been made keenly aware of their existence and familiar with many of their characteristics. The animals were very much a part of the children's conceptual worlds. Through the intervention of language, children who had never seen the animal were still able to have it as a part of their worlds. What is more (as we saw there), whether or not the animal was real in the absolute sense was irrelevant. It would have made no difference if, instead of an animal, the creature in question had been a supernatural spirit. It would still have been just as much a part of the child's world.

Thought affects Language

Language, therefore, affects thought, but thought also can affect language. The point is that, although our language does influence our perception, it does not do so to the extent that we cannot overcome it if there is sufficient motivation for us to make the effort. It does suggest interpretations of sense data, and no doubt most of what most people say is very much in conformity with what is easiest to say — the easiest interpretation. And, as we have said, there can be no doubt that what we perceive when we do *not* talk tends to be influenced in the same way.

But we can escape the influence, and we can modify our language by introducing new concepts or metaphors whenever it becomes apparent that they would serve a useful purpose. This is a standard practice in scientific, information-processing, and public relations professions. In general, to do so is likely to give the impression of a 'fresh' perspective, one which is less trite, albeit doubtless more taxing for the audience, than the usual utterance.

Moreover, in the long range, perspective languages are, in the words of Dell Hymes, 'what their users have made of them', that is, each language is the artefact of the uses to which it has been adapted.[1] Each conceptual world is essentially the product of the construction, in the process of language use, of a large number of conceptual events over a long period of time. Many languages of Asia and other parts of the third world are right now undergoing enormous changes which are consequent upon their being called upon to provide translations of scientific, social-scientific, legal, etc., works originally written in European languages. So far from being immovable impediments to the thought of their speakers, they are being reshaped by those speakers at a dizzying rate.[2]

Grammar vs. Vocabulary

One factor which has contributed to the mystifying character which the language and thought issue has assumed has been the particular model of language structure to which linguistic science has been committed. In this model all of the features which signal relations among elements in the sentence are seen as associated together in a single system — the syntactic system — and, further-more, that system is considered to represent the essence of the language. This particular perspective of linguistic science has made it possible to acknowledge that there is a strong relation between the *vocabulary* of a language and the thought of its speakers without acknowledging that the real *essence* of the language is in any way implicated. Furthermore, it has caused the characteriza-tions of languages produced by linguistics to remain on so abstract a level that a language can undergo what at least in the experience of its speakers is very rapid and fundamental change (as many Third-World languages are doing right now), and yet this change can almost entirely elude linguistic analysis of the traditional kind.[3]

Still, it is presumably necessary to say something here about the effect of grammar, in the strict sense (i.e. not including the meanings of lexical items), on thought and of thought on grammar. As regards the effect of grammar on thought, it has been suggested that what have been called the 'compulsory categories' of a language exercise an influence on the thought processes, especially the perception, of its speakers.[4] We may imagine that having to pay overt attention to some particular aspect of the situation probably does have some effect, but that the magnitude of the effect probably varies from one individual to another and from one category to another.

For one thing, some grammatical compulsory categories represent rather straightforward semantic choice (e.g. English singular vs. plural). In such cases one is required to pay particular overt attention to the relevant aspects of the situation being reported. However, other compulsory categories seem to reflect arbitrary grammatical requirements with no semantic content (e.g. grammatical gender, and noun classes generally, often hardly deserve whatever semantic labels they may conventionally be given (consider, for example, French *amour*, *délice*, and *orgue*, which are masculine in the singular and feminine in the plural). It is unclear how the necessity to observe such distinctions could affect the speakers' perception. Other compulsory choices fall in between; for example, verbs or prepositions governing particular cases in their objects (e.g. German *über* and *in* govern the accusative when signifying movement, but the dative when signifying location; *wegen* and others govern the genitive), or choice of prepositions (e.g. German *mit einer gewissen Geschwindigkeit*, '*with* a certain speed' (vs. Eng. 'at').

As regards the effect of thought on grammar, the main point to be made seems to be that thought as manifested in language use does seem to exert some effect on the syntactic means available in languages as well as on the patterns of their use. For example, it seems that the following kinds of changes are likely to occur in the process of language 'modernization': (1) more abstract terms, (2) changes in derivational morphology, one aspect of which is the addition of, or expanded use of, affixes which nominalize verbs, (3) more conjunctions, (4) introduction of, or extended use of, passive constructions.[5]

Conclusion

It seems that actually much of the effect of language on thought and of thought on language is to be found in the ways of talking rather than in the most rigidly conventionalized parts of the language. It appears that the entering wedges of much linguistic change are to be found there. This discussion has, of course, been a very sketchy one by comparison with the importance of the problem. However, I hope it has been sufficient to show that the relation between language and thought is not the intractable matter that the literature sometimes suggests it to be.[6]

Notes

1. Hymes' statement that languages are 'what their users have made of them' is from Hymes 1974: 206.
2. We might say that thought negotiates with the existing linguistic resources. The following quotation from Charles F. Hockett is relevant:

> . . . it is worthy of note that the history of Western logic and science, from Aristotle down, constitutes not so much the story of scholars hemmed in and misled by the nature of their specific languages as the story of a long and successful struggle against inherited linguistic limitations. (Hockett 1954: 122)

3. Edward Sapir is often invoked to support the distinction between vocabulary and the essence of the language. Sapir wrote (1921: 234), 'It goes without saying that the mere content of language is intimately related to culture,' and further on, 'The linguistic student should never make the mistake of identifying a language with its dictionary.'
4. Franz Boas and his followers were particularly interested in compulsory categories. Cf., for example, Boas 1911; cf. also Grace 1981: 44–6.
5. There is not much literature on the subject of the kinds of grammatical changes that are associated with 'modernization'. I have been influenced by Alisjahbana 1965 and Lichtenberk 1979.
6. Whorf also has made the point that the mutual effects of language and thought are to be sought in the ways of talking. He said (Carroll 1956: 158):

> Concepts of 'time' and 'matter' are not given in substantially the same form by experience to all men but depend upon the nature of the language or languages through the use of which they have been developed. They do not depend so much upon ANY ONE SYSTEM (e.g., tense, or nouns) within the grammar as upon the ways of analyzing and reporting experience which have become fixed in the language as integrated 'fashions of speaking' and which cut across the typical grammatical classifications, so that such a 'fashion' may include lexical, morphological, syntactic, and otherwise systematically diverse means coordinated in a certain frame of consistency.

10

The Question of
Individual Linguistic Competence

Considerable discussion has been evoked by Noam Chomsky's characterization of linguistics as a branch of cognitive psychology.[1] Although there is much to be said for the objection that that conception of the discipline leaves social factors too much out of account, it seemingly must be agreed that individual human beings as the users of language are its ultimate physical *locus*.

It seems, therefore, that our knowledge of the phenomenon, language, cannot ever be complete unless we understand how language manifests itself in these individuals. Although, the ultimate form of such knowledge must reflect its manifestations in the nervous systems of the individuals, the attainment of that kind of knowledge seems still far in the future. What can serve as a more realistic immediate objective, however, is a theory of the individual which explains (i.e. provides a model of) the actual competences displayed.

It would seem, then, that the first step toward constructing an explanatory theory should be to determine what kinds of competence are manifested in the linguistic behavior of individuals — that is, to determine empirically the facts that our theory is to undertake to explain. However, it is easy to show that we have so far failed to give our direct attention to the nature of linguistic competence, and that that failure has been due primarily to the dominant position occupied by the *langue* concept in linguistic theory generally. According to the '*langue*' concept language is divided up (without remainder) into a number (in fact, an undeterminable number) of distinct systems, the individual languages. It is these languages, the '*langues*' of Ferdinand de Saussure, which have been the object of linguistics.[2] Linguistics has been the study, be it synchronic or diachronic, of their structures.

Linguistics has tacitly presupposed for the individual a linguistic role limited almost entirely to serving as a repository for the *langue*. And yet, as we saw, the *langue* is a fiction (in the sense in which an open system is a fiction) whereas the individual is not. Therefore, there is an evident need for a complementary approach which takes the individual linguistic competence as prior and then regards the *langue* in the light of this competence. That is, we should consider the individual as the possessor of certain inherent capacities and of certain acquired skills and knowledge. And we should recognize that language in the final analysis consists just in those linguistically relevant capacities, skills, and knowledge of the individual. But in order to see them clearly, we need to free ourselves from the perspective in which the only things which attract our notice are those which are relevant to the problem of linguistic description as we now conceive of it.

A theory of the linguistic competence of the individual should be of considerable interest well beyond the field of linguistics proper. The central question might be defined as that of determining what characteristics it would be necessary to design into a machine in order to simulate the linguistic abilities of human individuals. A theory of competence should offer much that would be pertinent to problems such as that posed by interaction with computers, and it should also be a rich source of suggestions for artificial-intelligence simulation. (In actual fact, it seems that research workers in the field of artificial intelligence are, on their own, making most of the progress toward a general theory of competence.)[3] But from the viewpoint of linguistics alone, the role played by the speaker as the repository of linguistic competence and therefore as the actual *locus* of language would in itself seem to provide sufficient justification for such a theory.

This chapter will consist in the main of suggestions as to what a theory of competence will ultimately have to include or to account for. It should be apparent that much of what is said will be quite speculative. We will begin with a few general suggestions, and then, consider the characteristics displayed by the individual in the capacities, respectively, of receiver and of transmitter of linguistic utterances.

Some General Suggestions about Competence

The first suggestion to be made is that linguistic competence consists ultimately of a variety of skills and a memory of experiences in which the verbal competent has no separate status. The skills are those which have developed out of the experience of solving various problems of language use. They include the physical skills involved in pronunciation, especially conspicuous in fluent pronunciation. They also include skills of other kinds. Examples would be (1) skills of 'hearing' a particular language — of extrapolating from limited clues so as to recognize what has been said, (2) skills of construing experiences in terms of the subject-matter-consecrated ways of talking provided by the linguistic repertoire available for the individual's use, and (3) skills of translation (especially increasing one's ability to find quasi-isomorphic solutions), as one accumulates a store of solved problems of translation.

These skills, themselves, involve a kind of memory. That linguistic competence involves a memory of experiences in which verbal and non-verbal elements are mingled seems to be confirmed by what we introspectively experience when asked to judge whether or not a proposed sentence is acceptable to say in our language or dialect or when asked to explain the meaning of a word.

The experience of testing the hypothetical sentence, as generally reported, is not one of consulting some stored linguistic description, but rather of searching for relevant contexts where such a sentence might appropriately be used. The experience of attempting to explain a word meaning is similar, except that contexts will, in fact, be found (assuming that one knows the word at all) and that one must then attempt to construct some kind of generalization to account for the set of contexts found. (That is supposing that one plays fair and does not succumb to the temptation of asking for the whole context along with the word. Given the context, of course, one can attempt a paraphrase of the whole sentence so as avoid the task of constructing a general theory of the meaning of the word.)

But what has so far been said would seem to suggest that (in glaring contrast to the economy customarily assumed in linguistic theory) human language users do not display any generalizations at all in their linguistic skills and knowledge. That is certainly not the case. Among the skills, there are certainly various complex processes which are 'facilitated' or 'grooved' so as to be efficiently repeatable. And knowledge is certainly 'chunked' in various ways.[4] In short, individuals consciously or unconsciously recognize the existence of various sorts of equivalences in sounds, meanings, structures, etc., and sometimes behave accordingly. However, it is also important to be aware that not all individuals — even those whose competence is based upon exactly the same inventory of languages and dialects — will recognize the same equivalences. It is also important to realize that the recognition of a chunk does not mean that the components of the chunk are no longer available separately. All human beings presumably display in some measure a tendency to erudition, i.e. to the accumulation of separate bits of knowledge, and a tendency to generalization, i.e. to grouping the separate bits in more or less sophisticated ways into larger chunks.

In discussing the linguistic sign we saw that a sign may be simultaneously motivated (i.e. composed of separately identifiable bits) and conventionalized (i.e. identified as a chunk). What that meant, in fact, was that the sign was presumed to be known both analytically (whence, motivated) and holistically (whence, conventionalized) by the speakers (i.e. by whatever sample of speakers is required by the particular descriptive theory in order for the sign to be attributed to the *langue*). Thus, from the point of view of the individual we may expect that, in addition to those signs which he/she knows only holistically or only analytically, there will be a large number which he/she knows simultaneously in both ways.[5]

There are a few other general points to make about individuals. First, they vary in ability in various ways.[6] Some idea of the dimensions along which differences exist and the range of individual differences is needed for an adequate theory of linguistic competence. There has still been conspicuously little attention to this problem.

Secondly, it is necessary to recognize that linguistic competence is not all assignable to a particular language. Individuals may quite normally be multilingual. Multilinguals may be expected to have a great deal of knowledge which must surely count as linguistic, but which specifies relations, equivalences, and the like *between* languages rather than being within any single language. Furthermore, individuals have idiosyncracies, some of which must on all other counts qualify as linguistic, but which cannot be interpreted as belonging properly to any particular language.

The Individual as Receiver

In the chapter on translation, we saw that all translation except isomorphic translation required that the translator begin by understanding what had been said. The fact is of course, that understanding is a necessary step in all communicative transactions. However, understanding in the sense intended here — understanding of what the sayer was *saying* — has been little studied.

There is, on the other hand, a great deal of current research on what the sayer was *doing* in saying what he/she did, or to put it differently, on why the sayer said it — what purpose the saying was intended to serve.[7] Some of this research deals with the role of metalinguistic clues which may help the audience in its attempt to perceive what the sayer is up to.[8] Such clues, of course, contribute importantly to the schema of the audience as it confronts the speech act, and thus to the way the speech act is perceived. The interpretation of the speech acts (as well as of other significant acts) of the participants in any kind of group interaction is, of course, an essential aspect of the interaction process. This interpretation, like much else involved in the use of language, is ordinarily an act of perception.

Understanding in the sense with which we are concerned here — understanding of what the sayer *said* rather than what he/she *did* — is also normally an act of perception. J. P. Thorne has pointed out that the experience which one has of 'hearing' sentences in a language which one knows is quite different from any experience available to someone who is exposed to the same auditory stimuli but who does not know the language. He reminds us that when we hear an ambiguous sentence (his example is 'I dislike playing cards'), we experience it, not at once as ambiguous, not in an indeterminate confounding of the two meanings, but in one particular interpretation. Or, more properly, we hear it in one interpretation at a time, because it may switch abruptly from one interpretation to another, and then back again. Thorne notes the similarity of this experience to that of looking at a Necker cube, where we see the cube either from above or from below, but cannot actually perceive it in both attitudes at the same instant.

The point is, once again, that in understanding an utterance, we do not first somehow register sensory data and then subsequently interpret the data in a separate act. On the contrary, the understanding is normally a single instantaneous act.[9]

A second, closely related, point is that we often seem to have only a very superficial and transient experience of the utterance itself, and simultaneously to experience its meaning directly. In the words of Berkeley, 'We act in all respects as if we heard the very thoughts themselves.'[10] Michael Polanyi has spoken of the 'transparency' of unexceptionable and easily understood texts, and noted that texts become relatively 'opaque' — i.e. that their form obtrudes upon our awareness — only if they present difficulties to our understanding or contain misspellings or other attention-attracting features.[11]

The Phenomenon of being 'Tuned In'

It seems obvious that the way in which the hearer's attention is directed is an important factor in the overall process of understanding. However, more than just attention in a narrow sense is involved. We are dealing, in fact, with complex perceptual schemata. It is apparent that we have schemata which in some fashion prepare us to 'hear' a particular language or dialect or even a particular speaker. We might speak of this as being 'tuned in' to that particular speaker, dialect, or language. This phenomenon is brought sharply to our notice by experiences such as the kind of mental scrambling we undergo when we are tuned in to one language and are, to our surprise, addressed in another.

One kind of case which would seem to be particularly illuminating for a theory of individual linguistic competence would be that of listening to a language or dialect which one has only partially learned. The effective schemata in such cases seem to be potentially quite complex. It seems that one responds on the basis of what one has learned of the language or dialect in question in so far as that reaches, but also that some sort of back-up pools of linguistic knowledge, not specific to the language or dialect in question, are available and come more or less spontaneously into play. It is surely an over-simplification of a complex subject simply to suggest (as is sometimes done) that one's mother tongue *interferes* in such cases. It is an oversimplification on both counts. First, to call it 'interference' suggests that the 'interfering' language forces itself upon the hapless subject willy nilly. In fact, the person may be casting about frantically for any suggestion which will bring what he/she is hearing into some sort of focus — eagerly grasping, as it were, at any potential source of 'interference'.

Secondly, it is also an over-simplification because the back-up knowledge does not necessarily come from the hearer's mother tongue. In fact, one gets the impression that some people tend to the opposite extreme, at least at times. That is, we seem sometimes to observe tendencies for people to confuse all of their *foreign* languages with one another. Moreover, people sometimes seem to expect one foreign language to provide better clues as to how to interpret something said in another foreign language than would their native language. Has it something to do with knowledge of all languages learned later in life being, in some way, of the same kind and different from the kind of knowledge which one has of one's mother tongue?[12]

Understanding something said in an imperfectly known language is still normally an act of perception, but the schemata behind such perceptions must be quite complex. Cases of interference of the classical kinds would, of course, constitute part of the evidence in a study of this phenomenon. For example, words in different languages which are comparable in form (usually cognates or loans) but more or less different in meaning have sometimes been labeled 'false friends' because they often mislead the foreign language learner into error.

But what is actually behind the 'false friends' phenomenon? Even if French *convenance* does remind us of 'convenience', why should that prevent our keeping separate in our memories what we know specifically about *convenance* and specifically about 'convenience'? I grant, of course, that we may find it expedient to draw upon what we know about 'convenience' to supplement our limited knowledge about *convenance* upon occasion. However, we often are not sure whether we are doing so or not. It is not clear why we cannot tell that we are doing so — why we sometimes find it impossible to distinguish the cases when we are relying upon our knowledge of *convenance* from those when we are resorting to our knowledge of 'convenience'. What does this experience say about the nature of our knowledge of language, about what it is that we know and in what form we store it?

The Act of Understanding

By the act of understanding I mean the act of perceiving (or should I call it 'registering'? — or 'taking account of'?) what an utterance means. We have so far been dealing with preliminaries, with the preparation of the receiver for the act of perception which he/she will be called upon to perform. That crucial act of perception involves the conversion of the meaning of the utterance being understood into some kind of cognitive representation.

In attempting to analyze this conversion, we are immediately confronted by the fact that we know nothing of the form of cognitive representations. However, let us very tentatively propose that we can distinguish at least three different ways in which we are able to treat something which has been said to us — three different kinds of representations of the same thing said. Two of these can properly be said to be representations of its 'content'.

1) The first kind of representation is a verbatim representation. That is, we remember the exact words that were said (actually, I think this should be loosened a bit to include a verbatim representation of the key words and the key grammatical relations with some latitude on the other details). I think we usually employ this (rather onerous) kind of representation when the form of the utterance has somehow obtruded upon our awareness. For example, there might have been something particularly remarkable about the form — the pronunciation, a pun, or something of the sort.

However, this kind of representation is also used precisely to *avoid* the responsibility of understanding. By resorting to this stratagem we are able to report to B what A has said without assuming the responsibility for interpreting it. We say to B in effect, 'These were his/her words; you do the understanding for yourself.' We can also employ this strategy for our own mental records — we can take care (because it does require a special effort) to remember the exact wording, or selected parts of it, because we do not understand it or are not sure that we understand it correctly, and so hold the final understanding in abeyance.

2) The second kind of representation does separate out the meaning, or at least what is perceived to be its gist, and represent it only. A fairly pure form of this kind of representation is suggested when we report in our own words a message which was delivered to us orally or in a letter or other written instrument. I say that it is 'suggested' because no verbal report necessarily gives an accurate representation of all that may be in the mind of the speaker. But it is certainly a familiar experience to understand perfectly well, or at least feel that we understand perfectly well, something that has been said — to feel that we

understand it well enough that there is no need to concern ourselves with remembering anything about the wording used in
the original utterance. This second kind of representation is that
which naturally reflects this kind of understanding.

3) The third kind of representation not only separates the
meaning out from the form but goes a step further and breaks
down the meaning into components which are incorporated into
what we might call our *archive*. That is, we retain the information contained in the utterance but without any record of how
we acquired that information.

The archive, in fact, is a sort of 'world schema' — our system
of storing what we know (or think we know, or suspect, etc.)
about the world we live in. It is a kind of memory store, and it is
from this store that the particular schemata which are operative
in acts of perception are drawn. (Very roughly, what I mean is
that I suppose that we remain constantly aware in some degree
of what kind of circumstances we are in, and in fact, that we are
continually deciding what the circumstances are and reporting
those decisions back to the archive, which then delivers up
appropriate schemata.)

The archive in this conception is not just a store of isolated
bits of information. Rather it contains assimilated (more or less)
information. I think also that it does not contain only information which has been received in linguistic form, nor is such
information segregated within the archive from information
deriving from other sources. It is the archive which accounts for
our knowing, for example, that James Madison was the fourth
president of the United States (although we may never have
been told that particular fact but rather can deduce it from other
facts that we know, e.g. that Madison followed Jefferson, who
followed Adams, who followed Washington, who was first) or,
for another example, that turtles cannot fly.[13] I suppose that
most people, at least in our society, would agree that they know
that turtles cannot fly, but that most have never actually had
that bit of information imparted to them in any direct way. It is,
rather, the kind of information that the archive can generate.

A final point to be made about the three kinds of cognitive representation which have been distinguished here is that they may not
be as separable in reality as they are in this analysis. In fact, it
seems clear that in representing even a single utterance to ourselves we often employ cognitive representations of more than one

of the three kinds. We may, for example, remember one or two specific words but only the general idea expressed by the rest of the utterance (thereby mixing kinds (1) and (2)). Or again we may, when we are not fully confident of our source of information, incorporate information into our archive but with some sort of special indication like, 'This may be a fact; X told me that it was, but it is in need of further confirmation' (mixing kinds (2) and (3)).

The Individual as Sayer

It was mentioned above that an experienced sayer displays skills in pronunciation and in construing experiences in terms of the subject-matter-consecrated ways of talking provided by the linguistic repertoire available to him/her. Here we will consider the sayer's task in a broader context — the general context of language use.

First of all we must take into account that speech like any other form of human behavior cannot be fully understood without our recognizing that people have (constantly) purposes. Furthermore, they devise and continually revise, mostly quite unconsciously, strategies to be used in pursuing their purposes. Particular strategies, of course, often embrace a number of different purposes simultaneously. A single act may, therefore, be motivated by a number of different purposes (in varying degrees).

Finally, having set purposes for themselves and having devised strategies to pursue them, people are furthermore capable of implementing those strategies (with greater or lesser degrees of efficiency, of course). A speech act, then, placed in its proper context, is part of the implementation of a strategy which has been designed to further the pursuit of one or more of the speaker's purposes.

It should be emphasized again that the actual content of the linguistic expression used is not necessarily of major importance in the overall strategy which is being implemented. Sometimes the strategy requires little more than that one avoid remaining silent. Or saying something may be simply a necessary prerequisite for the encoding of sociolinguistic information. Or again the role in the overall strategy of what one chooses to say may be quite distinct from anything that could be inferred from its face value.

We saw above that the content of a linguistic expression includes a conceptual event, a modality, and clues as to what contextualization was intended for them. Because of the contextualization itself, therefore, the actual linguistic expression has to be tailored to the intended audience. However, there is more than that to designing the linguistic expression. The sayer is pursuing his/her purposes, and the strategy for accomplishing those purposes does not turn only upon what is to be said (i.e. what information is to be conveyed) but actually involves a whole expository strategy. Such strategies involve matters such as what is highlighted and what is played down, what is asserted and what is presupposed, and whatever else may promise to make the utterance more persuasive to the target audience. These strategies are of considerable importance to any complete understanding of how language works — particularly to any attempt to predict utterances in advance or even to explain *post hoc* why a specific linguistic expression was used.[14]

Expository strategies will play a part from the choice of model (i.e. of the conceptual event) on, since the choice of model is important, for example, in what is highlighted or what is presupposed. They will even play a part in the choice of elements, since not all elements made available by the language will be known to all potential audiences, or if known, be remembered with the same degree of favor or disfavor.

How much to say or to leave unsaid — i.e. how much information to provide and how much to leave to the audience to supply — is also partly a matter of expository strategy. We may say that the starting point is a basic rule that one should attempt to provide all and only the information that is necessary. To give too little information, of course, may simply lead to loss of interest by the audience (who do not understand what one is talking about) or, alternatively, to a jumping to a possibly wrong conclusion on their part. Or, again, if the audience is sufficiently motivated, it can lead to a protracted negotiation to arrive at the meaning intended. On the other hand, to give too much information can again lose the interest of the audience (who become bored), and is likely to be perceived as patronizing if not outright insulting.

The role of this aspect of expository strategy involves many more complications than the present discussion can do justice to. The device of leaving a bit unsaid so that understanding is not immediate can achieve several purposes. It can contribute to a sense of satisfaction in the audience once understanding has occurred — satisfaction that one has successfully met the challenge of catching on. It can also lead to a sense of solidarity with the sayer ('You and I have so much in common that we can understand each other even when much is left unsaid.'). Incomplete information in this sense is an important element in wit; it is generally regarded as sophisticated. There are other kinds of styles, however, which make deliberate use of redundancy of information. This seems to function as a means of giving added elaboration and hence added weight to a point. Some styles of oratory come to mind as examples.

Another kind of decision as to how much information to provide must also be mentioned. This kind of decision goes back to another aspect of the sayer's purpose, namely, what degree of exactitude does that purpose require in the information which he/she intends to communicate? For example, will giving an answer in round numbers provide insufficiently exact information, or would failing to round the numbers off give the impression, in the particular context, of over-fastidious exactitude? If exactitude is required, how much exactitude? Should we say that A is 60 miles from B, or 62 miles, or 61.73246 miles? Each choice suggests something slightly different about the sayer's purpose, about what the sayer is up to. But this is actually just a special case of the problem of choosing an appropriate degree of goodness of fit between conceptual events and real-world situations which was the subject of an earlier chapter.

The competence required in the role of sayer is also very complex, then. It ranges from knowledge of the conceptual world of the language to an empathic understanding of the character of the audience as well as of its mental set at the moment of speech. And skillful performance in the role requires not only a fine-grained appreciation of both but a skill in orchestrating all of the variables into an artful unity.

Conclusions

This chapter has been intended to show that if the actual *locus* of language is in the individual human beings who use it, the form which it assumes there is quite different from that which we tend to attribute to it. In fact, we have tended to think of the linguistic competence of an individual as being nothing more than replicas of linguistic descriptions of one or more *langues* (usually one). I suggest that the *langue* concept has been a principal source of distortion in our perception of language.

Here we have raised the question of what kinds of skills and knowledge would have to be designed into a machine in order to simulate human linguistic competence. The answer, in part, seems to be that those skills and knowledge are many and varied, and that many of them are not discontinuous with skills and knowledge required for various extra-linguistic competences of the individual. Among other things, language seems to involve memory which comprises cognitive representations of different kinds, and we seem to be capable of tuning ourselves in in such a way as to have different kinds of access to this memory store. We are capable of manipulating complex interactions involving incoming sensory information, the memory stores to which we have at that moment various degrees of access, and our own current purposes.

Although what has been said here suggests that linguistic competence as a whole is in no sense a neatly delimited domain within the human individual, that conclusion, although it might indicate that linguistics has much to learn from neighboring sciences, also suggests that language occupies a crucial and extensively ramified place in human psychology and that linguistics may likewise have much to teach.

Notes

1. One of Chomsky's earliest references to linguistics' being a branch of cognitive psychology is to be found in Chomsky 1968: 1.

2. The concept of the '*langue*' comes from Saussure 1916.

3. An example of work in artificial intelligence which throws light on individual linguistic competence would be Schank 1982, which was mentioned above.

4. On the concept of 'chunking' see Miller 1956: 92 and Simon 1974.

5. For the notion of 'holistic' and 'analytic' ways of knowing, cf. Grace 1981: 19 and *passim*.

6. One recent book which is directed at the problem of individual differences in linguistic competence is Fillmore *et al.* 1979.

7. The question of what the sayer was *doing* involves speech-act theory. Cf. for example, Austin 1965, Searle 1969.

8. For clues used in inferring the sayer's intentions, see, for example, Schollon and Schollon 1981 and numerous works of John J. Gumperz — e.g. Gumperz 1977, 1982a, b.

9. The discussion of 'hearing' sentences is found in Thorne 1966.

10. As quoted in Thorne 1966: 8.

11. The Polanyi references are to Polanyi 1958: 91 and 57.

12. Some of the work of Walter J. Ong suggests that knowledge of all

languages learned later in life is of the same kind, as contrasted with the knowledge of one's mother tongue (cf. Ong 1977: 27 – 8, for example).

13. Daniel C. Dennett (1978) in various places discusses kinds of things which we know and how we know them (cf. 1978: 45, 111, 132).

14. As I have mentioned earlier, I find the approach to expository strategy in Fowler *et al*. 1979 and Kress and Hodge 1979 particularly promising.

Concluding Remarks

The thesis of this book is that we — our culture in general and the science of linguistics in particular — have a false view of the nature of language. According to this thesis the realities in which we human beings effectively live our lives are realities which we have constructed, and language is the primary instrument of such reality construction. It is suggested, furthermore, that reality construction is probably to be regarded as the primary function of human language.

But the view of language which underlies this thesis itself represents an act of reality construction. Language has not customarily been conceived of in this way. This 'reality-construction' view of language contrasts with the traditional view, which in this book is called the 'mapping' view, and by the same token, the 'language' of this reality-construction view contrasts with the 'language' of the mapping view.

It is very important to recognize that differences between subject-matter views, even though they may appear from some perspectives to be slight, can have exceedingly important implications. It is true, for example, that a plausible case might be made that the differences between the mapping and reality-construction views of language are insignificant. It might be argued that they essentially agree on the main conditions governing the representation of reality by language. Both agree that such representation is to some extent dictated by common constraints imposed by the nature of the real world. They likewise agree that it is also to some extent a matter of interpretation, and that the interpretation has considerable freedom to differ from one language (or linguistic repertoire) to another. Thus, one might contend that both have essentially the same conception (and an unexceptionable one at that) of the relation between language and the real world which language in some sense represents.

However, we saw that the differences which do exist between the two views, however trifling they may at first appear, have extremely important implications. The mapping view gives precedence to the constraints imposed by the real world. It assumes that the resulting linguistic representations are *close enough* to being a direct reflection of the character of the real world that the sets of possible realities which different languages are capable of representing are to all intents and purposes the same. Consequently, it assumes that any potential reality which can be represented in one language can be represented in any other one. That assumption is what we have been calling the *intertranslatability postulate*. The reality-construction view does not make that assumption. In fact, as we saw in the book, it ultimately leads to the conclusion that the postulate is false — that there is no reasonable interpretation which can be given to it by which it would be true. (This does not mean, of course, that translation, sometimes quite exact, is not possible between languages which have the same *way of talking* about the subject matter in question. But the same subject matter and the same way of talking about it — or ways of talking which show detailed similarities — must be assumed to reflect either a common history or acculturation.)

It seems to follow, therefore, that the choice which we make between the two competing views of language has important implications not only for our understanding of what language is, but also for our understanding of the world we live in and the state of our knowledge of that world.

But if all of this is true, what should we do about it? If the reality-construction view of language is given serious consideration, it will probably have implications reaching in a number of different directions. For one thing, an investigation of the history of the intertranslatability postulate seems well worth undertaking. How, one might wonder, could such an idea conceivably arise? Where and how did someone come up with the idea that speaking produces a non-physical entity — a 'thing' which is only given physical substance by a linguistic expression in which it is 'encoded', but which is analytically separable from its physical expression? And how did it come to be imagined that this non-physical 'message' or 'meaning' could be extricated from its linguistic expression and then re-encoded intact into another linguistic expression?

Moreover, there will likely be implications for various other disciplines. The reality-construction view of language should provide the basis for a fresh look at the use of language in scientific and bureaucratic discourse and in information processing generally. The indications are that this fresh look might well lead to an altered understanding of the basis of science (especially perhaps, of such sciences as linguistics itself and the social sciences). In fact, the reality-construction view might even have something of interest to offer to those concerned with the foundations of mathematics and, for somewhat similar reasons, to those concerned with the simulation, by means of devices such as computers, of any kind of human functioning which in some way involves language.

Further, serious consideration of implications of the reality-construction view would surely lead to a fresh look at the machinery underlying the representational function of language in ordinary use, i.e. a look which would no longer take for granted the kind of machinery attributed to languages by the mapping view with its overriding concern with expository prose. This book has provided only the beginnings of an analysis of this machinery, but a fuller understanding of it seems likely to lead, in turn, to a fuller understanding of how language is used in discourse to shape an audience's perceptions of events and circumstances. The pervasive role of such uses of language in present-day political processes has, of course, been receiving steadily increasing attention of late.

There may also be grounds to hope that freeing ourselves from the notion of 'referential meaning' — the notion that there is a kind of 'meaning' possessed by a linguistic expression which consists in a set of constraints on what that expression may be used to refer to — can have a liberating effect on our attempts to understand language functions as a whole. For example, the view proposed in this book would seem to provide a better basis for studying the functioning of language in social interaction of all sorts — that is, for studying the ways in which particular linguistic features are exploited for what have been called 'social' and 'expressive' meaning. It even seems possible that the reality-construction view of language might have something to offer to those concerned with literary uses of language, or even more generally to humanities scholars who have need of a view of language suitable to serve as a foundation for their disciplines, but who have found that the dominant view of language in linguistics cannot be adapted for their purposes.

But perhaps the most important implications are the practical ones, and perhaps the best place to begin is with translation itself. Surely, a fresh look is needed at the problem of translation between languages — a fresh look in which an attempt is made to determine what is actually possible and how it is achieved, rather than simply assuming that the content of the source-language expression can be rendered in the target language — rather than assuming, that is, either that the target language can be made to accept some 'message' on the source language's own terms or that a rendering in the target language's own terms can do sufficient justice to an original source-language message.

And once something has been learned about what is possible and what is not, we should surely be prepared to examine the implications of what has been learned for the institutions of our society. For example, we should consider which of our institutions have established procedures for dealing with speakers of different languages or materials written in different languages, and examine those procedures to determine whether they make unrealistic assumptions, in terms of our new understanding of language, about what translations or the use of interpreters can accomplish.

Moreover, if, as this book has contended, it is not possible to produce an expression in a target language which accurately represents the content of a source-language expression, should we not ask ourselves about 'translation' between different ways of talking in the same language? Is that different in kind from translation between different languages? In fact, what may we reasonably assume about the ability of one speaker of a language to understand something said by another speaker of the same language when the two do not have access to the same ways of talking? Or when we have made no effort to determine whether they do or do not? And what are the implications of the answers to that question for our institutions? For example, do we have institutions which assume that if it is once established that a person is an English speaker, then that person can fairly be held responsible for understanding anything which is said (or presented in writing) to him/her in English? And do we have institutions which assume that English-speaking persons in some positions of authority are qualified to judge what any other English-speaking person means by anything he/she says in English?

And what of the concerns which ordinary citizens have with language? In addition to those whose professional, official, academic, or scientific responsibilities require that they make assumptions (conscious or unconscious) about the nature of language, there are all of those who have some direct practical interest. There are a large number of people in the world at any particular moment in time who, for one reason or another, find themselves in a place where some language other than their own is spoken. There are others who, while remaining at home, have regular dealings with speakers of other languages. Have we anything to say to them? It seems likely that the view of language developed here could eventually provide us with something of direct relevance to offer to people who for either of these reasons or for any other are forced to cope with language differences on a daily basis.

Finally, there is one last, and most general, concern. If the thesis of this book is correct, the extent to which translation between languages is possible corresponds to the extent to which cultural diversity has been suppressed. Linguists have long recognized that something is lost when a language disappears, that humankind is impoverished by each decrease in the linguistic diversity of the world. However, it follows from the thesis of this book that a still more serious loss is the loss of diversity *in the reality-construction sense.* That loss of diversity is marked, not so much by a decrease in the number of languages spoken in the world as by an *increase* in the extent to which the existing languages are intertranslatable. The extent to which intertranslatability increases is the extent to which all languages have become expressions of the same culture. And *that*, in turn, is the extent to which our accumulated cultural capital — our heritage from all of the preceding generations of humankind — has been dissipated.

References Cited

Aarsleff, Hans. 1982. *From Locke to Saussure: Essays on the study of language and intellectual history*. Minneapolis: University of Minnesota Press.

Alisjahbana, S. Takdir. 1965. New national languages: A problem modern linguistics has failed to solve. *Lingua 15*: 515–30.

Austin, J. L. 1963. Performative-constative. In Charles E. Caton (ed.). *Philosophy and ordinary language*. Urbana IL: University of Illinois Press, pp. 22–33.

———— 1965. *How to do things with words*. New York: Oxford University Press.

Bartlett, Frederic C. 1932. *Remembering: A study in experimental and social psychology*. Cambridge: Cambridge University Press.

Bateson, Gregory. 1972. *Steps to an ecology of mind*. New York: Ballantine Books.

Berger, Peter L., and Thomas Luckmann. 1966. *The social construction of reality: A treatise on the sociology of knowledge*. Garden City NY: Doubleday and Co., Inc.

Boas, Franz. 1911. Introduction. Handbook of American Indian Languages, Vol. 1. *Bureau of American Ethnology, Bulletin 40*. pp. 5–83.

Bolinger, Dwight. 1965. The atomization of meaning. *Language 41*: 555–73.

Carroll, John B. 1953. *The study of language*. Cambridge MA: Harvard University Press.

———— (ed.). 1956. *Language, thought, and reality: Selected writings of Benjamin Lee Whorf*. New York: John Wiley & Sons.

Chomsky, Noam. 1968. *Language and mind*. New York: Harcourt, Brace & World, Inc.

Cohen, Murray. 1977. *Sensible words: Linguistic practice in England, 1640–1785*. Baltimore: Johns Hopkins University Press.

Coleman, Linda and Paul Kay. 1981. Prototype semantics: The English word *lie*. *Language 57*: 26–44.

Conklin, Harold C. 1962. Lexicographical treatment of folk taxonomies. In Fred W. Householder and Sol Saporta (eds.). *Problems in lexicography*. *International Journal of American Linguistics vol. 28, no. 2, part. IV*, pp. 119–41.

Dennett, Daniel C. 1978. *Brainstorms: Philosophical essays on mind and psychology*. Montgomery VT: Bradford Books.

Downs, Roger M. and David Stea (eds.). 1973. *Image and environment: Cognitive mapping and spatial behavior*. Chicago: Aldine.

Eldredge, Niles, and Stephen Jay Gould. 1972. Punctuated equilibria: An alternative to phyletic gradualism. In Thomas J. M. Schopf (ed.). *Models in paleobiology*. San Francisco: Freeman, Cooper & Co., pp. 82–115.

Feuer, L. S. 1953. Sociological aspects of the relation between language and philosophy. *Philosophy of Science 20*: 85–100.

Fillmore, Charles J., Daniel Kempler, and William S-Y. Wang (eds.). 1979. *Individual differences in language ability and language behavior*. New York: Academic Press.

Fowler, Roger, Bob Hodge, Gunther Kress, and Tony Trew. 1979. *Language and control*. London, Boston & Henley: Routledge & Kegan Paul.

Frake, Charles O. 1961. The diagnosis of disease among the Subanon of Mindanao. *American Anthropologist 63*: 113–32.

—— 1962. The ethnographic study of cognitive systems. In Thomas Gladwin and William C. Sturtevant (eds.). *Anthropology and human behavior*. Washington: The Anthropological Society of Washington, pp. 72–85.

Gallwey, W. Timothy. 1974. *The inner game of tennis*. New York: Random House.

Gibson, James J. 1979. *The ecological approach to visual perception*. Boston, etc.: Houghton Mifflin Co.

Goffman, Erving. 1981. *Forms of talk*. Philadelphia: University of Pennsylvania Press.

Grace, George W. 1981. *An essay on language*. Columbia SC: Hornbeam Press.

Gumperz, John J. 1977. Sociocultural knowledge in conversational inference. In Muriel Saville-Troike (ed.). *Linguistics and anthropology. Georgetown University Round Table on Languages and Linguistics 1977*, pp. 191–211.

—— 1982a. *Discourse strategies*. Cambridge: Cambridge University Press.

—— (ed.). 1982b. *Language and social identity*. Cambridge: Cambridge University Press.

Head, Henry. 1920. *Studies in neurology*. 2 vols. London: Henry Frowde and Hodder & Stoughton, Ltd.

Hockett, Charles, F. 1954. Chinese versus English: An exploration of the Whorfian theses. In Harry Hoijer (ed.), *Language in Culture, American Anthropological Association, Memoir 79*, pp. 106–23.

Hoijer, Harry (ed.). 1954. Language in culture. *American Anthropological Association, Memoir 79*.

Hymes, Dell. 1960. Lexicostatistics so far. *Current Anthropology 1*: 3–44.

—— 1974. *Foundations in sociolinguistics: An ethnographic approach*. Philadelphia: University of Pennsylvania Press.

Jaynes, Julian. 1976. *The origin of consciousness in the breakdown of the bicameral mind*. Boston: Houghton Mifflin Company.

Jerison, Harry J. 1973. *Evolution of the brain and intelligence*. New York: Academic Press.

Katz, Jerrold J. 1972. *Semantic theory*. New York, etc.: Harper and Row, Publishers.

—— 1976. A hypothesis about the uniqueness of natural language. In Harnad, Stevan R., Horst D. Steklis, and Jane Lancaster (eds.). 1976. *Origins and evolution of language and speech. Annals of the New York Academy of Sciences, vol. 280*, pp. 33–45.

—— 1978. Effability and translation. In F. Guenthner and M. Guenthner-Reutter (eds.). *Meaning and translation*. New York: NYU Press, pp. 191–234.

―――― 1981. *Language and other abstract objects.* Totowa NJ: Rowman and Littlefield.

Kress, Gunther and Robert Hodge. 1979. *Language as ideology.* London, Boston & Henley: Routledge & Kegan Paul.

Kuhn, Thomas S. 1970. *The structure of scientific revolutions.* 2nd. ed. Chicago: University of Chicago Press.

Lakoff, George. 1972. Hedges: A study in meaning criteria and the logic of fuzzy concepts. *Papers from the eighth regional meeting of the Chicago Linguistics Society*, pp. 183–228.

―――― and Mark Johnson. 1980. *Metaphors we live by.* Chicago: University of Chicago Press.

Lenneberg, Eric H. 1953. Cognition and ethnolinguistics. *Language 29*: 463–71.

Lichtenberk, Frantisek. 1979. Syntactic iconism, coordination, subordination, and language evolution. *University of Hawaii Working Papers in Linguistics 11(2)*: 79–88.

Lyons, John. 1977. *Semantics.* 2 vols. Cambridge, etc.: Cambridge University Press.

Mandelbaum, David G. 1949. *Selected writings of Edward Sapir.* Berkeley & Los Angeles: University of California Press.

Miller, George A. 1956. The magical number seven, plus or minus two: Some limits on our capacity for processing information. *The Psychological Review 63*: 81–97.

Morris, Charles W. 1938. Foundations of the theory of signs. *International Encyclopedia of Unified Science, vol. 1, no. 2.* Chicago: University of Chicago Press.

Northrop, F. S. C. 1947. *The logic of the sciences and the humanities.* New York: Macmillan.

Olson, David R. 1977a. Oral and written language and the cognitive processes of children. *Journal of Communication 27(3)*: 10–26.

―――― 1977b. From utterance to text: The bias of language in speech and writing. *Harvard Educational Review 47(3)*: 257–81.

Ong, Walter J. 1977. *Interfaces of the word: Studies in the evolution of consciousness and culture.* Ithaca NY: Cornell University Press.

―――― 1982. *Orality and literacy: The technologizing of the word.* London and New York: Methuen.

Osgood, Charles E. and Thomas A. Sebeok (eds.). 1954. Psycholinguistics: A survey of theory and research problems. *International Journal of American Linguistics Memoir 10.*

Partridge, Eric. 1962. *A dictionary of clichés, with an introductory essay.* 4th edition, reprinted. London: Routledge & Kegan Paul Ltd.

―――― 1977. *A dictionary of catch phrases: British and American, from the sixteenth century to the present day.* New York: Stein and Day, Publishers.

Pawley, Andrew, and Frances Hodgetts Syder. 1983a. Two puzzles for linguistic theory: Nativelike selection and nativelike fluency. In Jack C. Richards and Richard W. Schmidt (eds.). *Language and Communication.* London and New York: Longman, pp. 191–225.

―――― 1983b. Natural selection in syntax: Notes on adaptive variation and change in vernacular and literary grammar. *Journal of Pragmatics 7*: 551–79.

References Cited

Pepper, Stephen C. 1957. *World hypotheses: A study in evidence.* Berkeley and Los Angeles: University of California Press.

Pike, Kenneth L. 1943. *Phonetics: A critical analysis of phonetic theory and a technic for the practical description of sounds.* Ann Arbor: The University of Michigan Press.

Polanyi, Michael. 1958. *Personal knowledge: Towards a post-critical philosophy.* Chicago: University of Chicago Press.

Quine, Willard Van Orman. 1960. *Word and Object.* New York etc.: John Wiley & Sons. (esp. Chap 2, Translation and meaning).

Reddy, Michael J. 1979. The conduit metaphor — a case of frame conflict in our language about language. In Andrew Ortony (ed.). *Metaphor and thought.* Cambridge: Cambridge Univeristy Press, pp. 284–324.

Rorty, Richard. 1979. *Philosophy and the mirror of nature.* Princeton NJ: Princeton University Press.

Rosch, Eleanor. 1975. Universals and cultural specifies in human categorization. In Richard W. Brislin, Stephen Bochner, and Walter J. Lonner (eds.). *Cross-cultural perspectives on learning.* New York: John Wiley & Sons, pp. 177–206.

Rosenberg, Jay F. 1981. On understanding the difficulty in understanding understanding. In Herman Parret and Jacques Bonveresse (eds.). *Meaning and understanding.* Berlin and New York: Walter de Gruyter, pp. 29–43.

Sapir, Edward. 1921. *Language: An introduction to the study of speech.* New York: Harcourt, Brace & Co.

Saussure, Ferdinand de. 1916. *Cours de linguistique générale.* Paris: Librairie Payot.

Schank, Roger C. 1982. *Reading and understanding: Teaching from the perspective of artificial intelligence.* Hillsdale NJ: Lawrence Erlbaum Associates.

Scollon, Ronald and Suzanne B. K. Scollon. 1979. *Linguistic convergence: An ethnography of speaking at Fort Chipewyan, Alberta.* New York: Academic Press.

———— 1981. *Narrative, literacy and face in interethnic communication.* Norwood NJ: Ablex Publishing Corporation.

Searle, John R. 1969. *Speech acts: An essay in the philosophy of language.* New York: Cambridge University Press.

Simon, Herbert A. 1974. How big is a chunk? *Science 183*: 482–8 (8 February).

Steiner, George. 1975. *After Babel: Aspects of language and translation.* New York and London: Oxford University Press.

Syder, Frances Hodgetts. 1983. *The fourth R: Spoken language, English teaching and social competence.* Palmerston North, New Zealand: Frances Hodgetts Syder.

Thorne, J. P. 1966. On hearing sentences. In J. Lyons and R. J. Wales (eds.). *Psychological papers: The proceedings of the 1966 Edinburgh Conference.* Edinburgh: University Press, pp. 3–10.

Tolman, Edward C. 1948. Cognitive maps in rats and men. *Psychological Review 55*: 189–208.

Uexküll, Jakob von. 1957. A stroll through the worlds of animals and men: A picture book of invisible worlds. (translated and edited by

References Cited

Claire H. Schiller — orig. Germ. edition, 1934). In Claire H. Schiller (ed.). *Instinctive behavior: The development of a modern concept.* New York: International Universities Press, pp. 5–80.

Vaihinger, H[ans]. 1968. *The philosophy of 'as-if': A system of the theoretical, practical and religious fictions of mankind.* (Translated by C. K. Ogden). New York: Barnes & Noble (orig. German edition published 1911).

Vinay, Jean-Paul and J. Darbelnet. 1958. *Stylistique comparée du français et de l'anglais: méthode de traduction.* Paris: Didier.

Weinreich, Uriel. 1962. Lexicographic definition in descriptive semantics. In Fred W. Householder and Sol Saporta (eds.).*Problem in lexicography. International Journal of American Linguistics, vol. 28, no. 2, part IV,* pp. 25–43.

Weinreich, Uriel. 1963. On the semantic structure of language. In Joseph H. Greenberg (ed.). *Universals of language.* Cambridge MA: The MIT Press.

Whitehead, Alfred North and Bertrand Russell. 1957. *Principia mathematica,* 2nd edition (2nd edition was originally published in 1925). Cambridge: Cambridge University Press.

Whorf, Benjamin Lee. 1950. *Four articles on metalinguistics* (Reprinted from *Technology Review* and from *Language, Culture, and Personality*). Washington DC: Department of State Foreign Service Institute.

Wittgenstein, Ludwig; 1958. *Philosophical Investigations.* Translated by G. E. M. Anscombe. 2nd ed. Oxford: Basil Blackwell.

Ziman, John. 1978. *Reliable knowledge: An exploration of the grounds for belief in science.* Cambridge: Cambridge University Press.

Zimmer, Karl E. 1971. Some general observations about nominal compounds. *Working Papers on Language Universals (May 1971).* Stanford CA: Stanford University Press.

Index

Adamic language (language of
 Adam) 14n4
archive 133
assumptions
 epistemological 4, 6, 17
 of science 12–13, 17, 21
 of subject-matter views 16–21
 of mapping view 6, 9–11,
  13, 25, 118
 of reality-construction view
  10–12, 25
 ontological 9, 82
 vs. beliefs 11, 19–20
Austin, J. L. 50
autonomous text 27, 41–4, 53,
 64
autonomy of linguistics 8

back-up knowledge 130–1
basic vocabulary 96
beliefs (vs. assumptions) 11,
 18–20
Bolinger, Dwight 49
bounded category 78

characterization (cf. sense) 60,
 76–90 passim, 98, 102,
 112–13
Chomsky, Noam 125
'close-enough' type of argument
 43, 139
cognitive representation 132–3,
 137
Coleman, Linda 48
commensurability 62–3, 68
communicative competence 92
compulsory categories 57, 59,
 123
conceptual element 33, 46–7,
 75–90 passim, 94–5, 98
conceptual event
 fit with real-world situation
  41–53 passim
 in contents of linguistic

expression 32–9 passim,
 75–6, 102
 instrument of change 113
 instrument of speaker strategy
  135
 nature of 31–6, 108
 translatability of 55–66 passim
conceptual world
 in individual competence 121,
  136
 nature of 75, 82, 108–13
  passim
 of a language-culture system
  11
 vis-à-vis conceptual event 31,
  34, 122
Condillac, Etienne Bonnet de 5
consensibility 103
consensual statement 104
content (of a linguistic
 expression)
 components of 34–9 passim,
  41, 55, 64
 identity of in translation 68
 nature of 25, 41, 45, 56
 relation to speaker's strategy
  134
constrained-reference conception
 of word meaning 76–7
contextualization (contextualization clues) 35–9, 55–6, 64,
  66, 95, 135
convergent development 106
culture(s) 5, 9–10, 70

Darbelnet, J. 57, 60
Destutt de Tracy, Antoine-Louis-
 Claude 5
discourse (ongoing) 17, 36–7
domain of experience 98–9

effective environment 3, 70, 75
empty code (languages as) 8
equivalences (cf. kinds) 80–2

expository strategy 64, 135

fit (between conceptual event
    and actual situation),
    goodness of 49–52
Frake, Charles 87

'hearing' a language 127, 129
Humboldt, Wilhelm von 5
Hymes, Dell 122

idiomaticity 105
idiomatology 93, 102
incorrigible (cf. problematic) 7,
    11, 118
'interference' 130
intertranslatability postulate
    implications for nature of
        language 8–9, 70
    key assumption of mapping
        view of language 7
    meaning of 28, 55, 66–8
    status of 12, 25, 56, 70, 140
isomorphic translation (vs.
    paraphrastic) 57–60, 62, 68

Johnson, Mark 98

Kay, Paul 48
kinds (cf. equivalences) 81–2
knowledge
    analytic 128
    'chunked' 128
    holistic 128
    of the world 92
Kuhn, Thomas S. 93, 100

Lakoff, George 49, 98
language-culture system 10–11
langue concept 125, 136
linguistic change 8, 124
linguistic competence 125–37
    passim
linguistic description(s) 8, 126
linguistic expression 25–38
    passim, 41–8 *passim*, 56–66
    passim, 135
linguistic repertoire
    and conceptual worlds 31,
        108, 111, 121

and thought 117
and ways of talking 98, 134
communication between
    different repertoires 70
conventional signs of 75

mapping view of language
    as standard view 4–5, 68,
        139
    consequent assumptions and
        implications 8–10, 141
    languages divide up the
        world 97
    underlying assumptions of
        6–7, 25–7, 41, 46,
        101–2, 139
    autonomous text 27, 64
    constrained-reference
        conception of word
        meaning 76, 78
    the intertranslatability
        postulate 7, 55, 68
    truth conditions 44–5
    status of 12–13, 20
    validity of 12–13, 38, 53, 63
metaphor
    particular 99, 112
    root 98–9, 112
modality (conditions of
    instantiation) 37–9, 55–6,
    64, 95, 135
models 6–7
modulation, fixed 60

nativelike selection 93
nature of language
    as concern of linguistics 16
    conceptions of
        errors in kind vs. errors of
            detail 43
        implications of 4
        invalidity of 117, 139
        mapping view 9–10
        reality-construction view
            10–11
non-adaptiveness (of features of
    language) 8

open systems 18–19, 99

paraphrastic translation (vs.

isomorphic) 57–63 *passim*, 93
Partridge, Eric 86
Pawley, Andrew 93
perlocutionary (conception of) intertranslatability 63–9 *passim*
Polanyi, Michael 130
problematic (cf. incorrigible) 7, 118

quasi-isomorphic translation 59–62, 127
Quine, Willard Van Orman 69

real world, reality 25–6, 30–1, 37, 42, 46
real-world situation 26–27, 41–9 *passim*, 55–6, 64
reality construction
by means of language 3–4, 139
conceptual events 25, 28, 31, 35, 38–9, 108
conceptual world 108
conventional signs 89
constructed realities
as effective environment 108, 139
as foundation of discourse 17
as models of reality 6
in conceptual events 31, 34
vs. actual reality 44–5
social 3
reality-construction view
and intertranslatability postulate 12, 25, 55
and subject-matter consecrated ways of talking 103–6
assumptions of 10–12, 117–18
conception of meaning 27, 41, 44, 46, 55–6, 77
contrasted with mapping view 4–7, 11–13, 16, 63, 101, 139–41
historical antecedents 5
Russell, Bertrand 37

Sapir, Edward 117
Saussure, Ferdinand de 125
sayable things 25, 27, 41
sayer
purpose of 136
role of 56, 64–5, 134
taker of responsibility 38, 40n4, 58, 95
saying something 25, 27–8, 38–9, 55
schemata 129–31, 133
semantic domain 104
sense (cf. characterization) 60, 75–89 *passim*, 98, 112
sensible world 110–11
sign
ad hoc 28, 76, 83–9 *passim*, 98, 102, 112–13
conventional 28, 75–6, 79, 83–9, 95, 98, 111–12
motivated 28, 76, 82–90 *passim*, 98, 112
sentence-level 28, 31, 76, 113
unmotivated 28, 76, 84–6
word-level 28, 76, 82, 113
signans 76, 82–9 *passim*, 95–8 *passim*, 106
signatum 76, 84, 87–9, 98
speech act 28, 31–2, 37–8, 65
subject matter 3, 97–106 *passim*, 112–13, 140
subject-matter views 16–21, 139
surrogate sayer conception of translator 67
Syder, Frances 93
syntactical structure (Carnapian concept of) 12

Thorne, J. P. 129
thought 5, 9–10, 70, 113, 117–24 *passim*
thought instrument 112
truth-conditional semantics 45, 53, 62
'tuned in', being 130, 136

Uexküll, Jakob von 109
Umwelten 109
understanding (of speech acts)

57 – 66 *passim*, 104, 129 – 33
passim, 142
universal encoder (languages as)
8 – 9, 53

Vaihinger, Hans 112
view(s) of language 4 – 6, 42 – 4,
55
Vinay, Jean-Paul 57, 60

way of talking
about commonplace things 29
construing experiences in
terms of 127, 134
development of 97, 112
different in same language
142

implications of 103 – 6
of modern world 70, 98
of scholarly traditions 19
same in different language
140
same or different subject
matter 99 – 102
structure of 98
Weinreich, Uriel 105
Whitehead, Alfred North 37
Whorf, Benjamin Lee 5, 61 – 2,
117 – 18
Wittgenstein, Ludwig 103
world view 5

Ziman, John 104